The Urban Campus

The Urban Campus
Educating the New Majority for the New Century

by
Peggy Gordon Elliott

AMERICAN COUNCIL
ON EDUCATION
Series on Higher Education
ORYX PRESS
1994

Copyright © 1994 by American Council on Education and The Oryx Press
Published by The Oryx Press
4041 North Central at Indian School Road
Phoenix, Arizona 85012-3397

Published simultaneously in Canada

Printed and Bound in the United States of America

∞ The paper used in this publication meets the minimum requirements of
American National Standard for Information Science—Permanence of
Paper for Printed Library Materials, ANSI Z39.48, 1984.

Library of Congress Cataloging-in-Publication Data
    The urban campus: educating the new majority for the new
century/by Elliott, Peggy G.
    p. cm.—(American Council on Education/Oryx series on
higher education)
    Published simultaneously in Canada.
    Includes bibliographical references and index.
    ISBN 0-89774-818-2
    1. Education, Urban—United States. 2. Education, Higher—
United States. I. Title. II. Series.
LC5131.E45 1994   94-5958
370.19'348—dc20   CIP

For Anne and Scotty and Mom

The United States is no longer an agrarian nation. It has become an urban nation. Most of its people live and work in urban agglomerations, fragmented perhaps into suburbs and inner cities, but nonetheless urban. For better or worse, the future of our country will largely be determined by the economic and social success or failure of its cities. Whether we and our children will enjoy success or suffer the consequences of failure depends critically on our ability to compete in the global economy and to live and work together in health and in peace. That ability in turn depends critically on the quality of the education available to our people, at all levels from kindergarten through postdoctoral. It also depends critically on our ability to find new approaches and solutions to old problems, and to bring that new found knowledge effectively to bear on our problems when and where they occur.

Donald N. Langenberg
Chancellor, the University of Maryland
From "A Voice from the Catacombs," an address to the University of Illinois Board of Trustees
9 March 1988

CONTENTS

❋ ❋ ❋ ❋ ❋ ❋ ❋ ❋ ❋

PREFACE

❋ ❋ ❋ ❋ ❋ ❋ ❋ ❋

The idea for a book on urban higher education first occurred to me in the late 1980s when, during my tenure as chancellor of Indiana University Northwest, I chaired the Coalition for Urban Higher Education and the American Association of State Colleges and Universities' Urban Affairs Committee. My growing involvement in urban higher education at the national level, which also included an active role as vice-chairperson of the American Association of Urban Universities, convinced me that urban campuses were sometimes being ignored because they did not fit neatly into the Carnegie Foundation's taxonomy of higher education or into any other popular classification such as U.S. News and World Report's annual ranking of institutions. In spite of a lack of conformity with more traditional ideas of education, the role of urban campuses in educating growing numbers of diverse populations was so significant that it required a fuller recognition and understanding. Moreover, interaction on a daily basis with an extraordinarily diverse student body caused me to realize that commonly held perceptions about the nature of higher education and the ways in which it should be delivered were often very unrealistic. Additionally, while enrollments at urban campuses have grown steadily, and sometimes phenomenally, public policy makers and legislative representatives sometimes had little idea of how these campuses operated or what their needs were.

Generally, I believe this lack of understanding is due to the fact that the representatives' and policy makers' own experience with higher education, like my own, was in a traditional setting. At age 18, just out of high school, our generation of youth left home to enroll in colleges, which were usually located in small towns some distance from any city. Along with our peers, we proceeded in steady progression through four years of undergraduate study. Nearly all of us were single, except for a few veterans attending with GI Bill support and living in special housing. Very few of us worked, except during summers or occasionally to pick up extra spending money.

We lived in a campus dormitory—noncoed (since the university also was expected to be a parent in absentia)—and we car-pooled or took the Greyhound home for brief family reunions during holidays. None of us thought of taking longer than four years to earn a bachelor's degree. We completed our undergraduate degrees, went to graduate school, attended our friends' weddings, became godparents to their children, and, because the economy was still in pretty good shape, had little difficulty in securing jobs.

While such a model of higher education, with some modifications, still exists for some young people today, ever-growing numbers of college students across the country do not fit this model. Many of these students are located, if not in the heart of a city, then on its periphery. Often, as is the case with the University of Houston in Texas and Miami-Dade Community College in Florida, urban universities have multiple campuses and enrollments of 30,000 to 40,000, sometimes more. The student mix, now frequently referred to as the New Majority, is very different as well. While dormitories do exist on many urban campuses, large numbers of students also live at home and commute to class. Some in the traditional 18- to 24-year-old age range live at home with their parents, while others have apartments. Among the older students, a sizable number are married or are single heads of households. Most New Majority students work, if not full-time, then part-time, and although many are dependent on some type of financial aid—a grant, loan, scholarship, or work-study arrangement—many are largely self-supporting and self-activated. The New Majority is characterized by its inordinate diversity—large numbers of women, minorities, displaced workers, career professionals returning to upgrade their skills, and senior citizens coming back for updated knowledge.

Despite a persistent perception of higher education as it "used to be," students of the urban era bear almost no resemblance to the image of the student in the fifties. For one thing, many of these students are place-bound by economic necessity or as the result of family obligations. Others simply prefer to live at home, work, be involved in various ways with the community, and attend a college that is near home. Most of them reside in metropolitan areas. Because New Majority students' lives are more complex, college may not be their number-one priority. Few of them graduate within the traditional four- or five-year span.

SCOPE

While this book discusses the advent and characteristics of the New Majority, its intent is much broader in scope. An unusually diverse mix of students is only one phenomenon that makes urban higher education distinct from traditional models. Major changes in the society—longer life-span, rapid technological development, intense global competition, shrinking resources, the passing of the machine age coupled with the birth of the information age, the shift from rural to urban—all have major implications for the delivery of higher education within the context of a society that is centered in cities. In a new era, with vastly differing and rigorous workplace demands, we cannot, with any degree of success, educate students while operating under the same assumptions and with the same models that were successful in the much different past. Urban campuses, and the New Majority that is served by them, present us with a variety of challenges, from the structuring of financial aid to help meet the needs of part-time students to the restructuring of the campuses for new delivery systems. Old assumptions about urban campuses, including those that claim that New Majority students require only the most basic of facilities and a limited range of academic degree programs, are called into question.

Much of the information presented in this book is anecdotal and is based, in part, on my own experiences first as a faculty member at an urban campus, later as a chancellor of an urban campus, and now as a president of an urban university. In preparing the manuscript, I encountered at least one major challenge. Despite the phenomenal growth of community colleges, many of which are located in or near cities, and the burgeoning enrollments of urban universities, there is not a substantial body of research and writing on urban higher education. With the exception of a few scholarly publications and an occasional book, information about urban campuses is quite sparse. While this book contributes to that body of knowledge, it also underscores the need for substantial research.

ARRANGEMENT

The book is organized in seven chapters. Chapter 1 focuses on changes in the society that have led to the development and growth of urban campuses and traces their emergence within the evolving framework of higher education in general. Chapter 2 attempts to set forth a broad definition of urban campuses: what they are and are not, what their mission is, their connections to the cities whose citizens they serve, and how they are sometimes misperceived. The third chapter discusses the New Majority: who they are; what their needs, goals, and expectations are; and some of the challenges they present to the standard "modus operandi" of higher education. Chapter 4 centers on urban faculty, a group that has been characterized as the "asphalt intelligentsia." It takes note of the challenges these faculty face from adult learners and classroom diversity, the ways in which their research often engages them with the urban milieu, benefits they gain from being located in metropolitan settings, and the broadened concept of scholarship they may be bringing to the academy.

Chapter 5 focuses on common frustrations of urban campuses, many of which are related to long-standing misconceptions about their role, their students, and their faculty. The chapter also explores misconceptions of governing bodies and accrediting agencies concerning urban campuses, inequities in funding, imposed limitations in academic programming, and misplaced fears related to territorial and competitive concerns within the academy.

Chapter 6 discusses the ways in which urban colleges and universities have played a key role in moving the society forward, not simply in terms of educating large and diverse numbers of citizens, but also in forging important developmental partnerships with business and industry, government and human service agencies, and public education. Among those partnerships cited are the Edison Polymer Innovation Corporation (EPIC), which links the University of Akron with Case Western Reserve University in Cleveland and 12 original corporate partners, whose number has now grown to approximately 70; and the Cheltenham school project in West Denver, where the Community College of Denver launched a program working with youngsters and their parents.

Chapter 7 sums up the great need for and urgency of urban higher education in preparing the nation's citizenry for the globally competitive and technologically complex world of the twenty-first century.

I wrote this book over a period of two years, beginning in the summer of 1991, when I was chancellor at Indiana University Northwest. I worked on it into the fall of 1993, after I had been installed as president of the University of Akron. I have written the book with administrators, faculty, and students in higher education in mind, as well as public policy makers, members of governing bodies, and many others who are interested in colleges that serve our cities.

Finally, I want to emphasize that the information presented in this volume does not suggest that any one institutional model is unimportant for its constituency. Rather, it asserts that one constituency—the more than three-quarters of American citizens who live in metropolitan areas—has grown greatly, will continue to grow, and therefore deserves the same consideration of its issues and needs as has been accorded others in higher education. Each of us in the field has a crucial role to play in educating this nation's citizens, in reviving the economy, and in moving our country toward a life of stability and quality in the century to come. To the extent that urban colleges and universities continue to be perceived as a threat to existing models rather than as an effective and critical resource for educating the growing New Majority, the effectiveness of the academy will be diminished. It is my great hope that this book will assist in clarifying existing, sometimes inaccurate, notions about urban campuses and will lead to a fuller understanding of their mission, their students, and their significant role in shaping this country's future.

ACKNOWLEDGMENTS

I am greatly indebted to all of those who worked with me in this endeavor and to all of the publications and scholars whose articles are quoted and whose works influenced this one. Among those publications that were particularly useful were *The New Realities* by Peter F. Drucker, *Megatrends 2000* by John Naisbitt and Patricia Aburdene, the "Urban Community Colleges Report" edited by Maurice D. Weidenthal, and a number of fine articles in the journal *Metropolitan Universities*, all of which are cited at the end of the chapters in which they are referenced. An article by Gary Orfield, "Public Policy and College Opportunity," first published by the University of Chicago and later by the *American Journal of Education*, was particularly helpful. Other books that provided background reading are *Scholarship Reconsidered: Priorities of the Professoriate* by Ernest L. Boyer, *The American Community College* by Arthur M. Cohen and Florence B. Brawer, *The Interactive University: A Source of American Revitalization* by J. Wade Gilley, *Involving Colleges* by George D. Kuh and others, *New Priorities for the University* by Ernest A. Lynton and Sandra E. Elman, *Higher Education in Partnership with Industry* by David R. Powers and others, *Faculty Lives: Vitality and Change* by E. Eugene Rice, and *Not Well Advised* by Peter Szanton. Of course, no bibliography of the literature on urban higher education would be complete without Maurice Berube's 1978 work, *The Urban University in America*. I also want to note the research on urban public universities by Mary K. Kinnick and Mary F. Ricks of Portland State University. Their excellent studies, which I understand are continuing, are among the few definitive research projects on urban higher education.

I want to acknowledge many people who assisted in and supported this work. This book would never have been completed without the extraordinary talent and help of Kay Rogers, associate director of public relations at the University of Akron and former colleague at Indiana University Northwest. Her years of excellent experience in university public relations, journalism, and editing enabled her to identify what the material lacked and to know just what to recommend in order to make it complete. I am personally enormously in her debt, and we are all fortunate that she chose to be a writer and to join our profession.

I also want to acknowledge the encouragement and assistance of Indiana University president Tom Ehrlich. When I doubted that it was possible to operate a campus and write a book simultaneously, he assured me that I could and found ways to help me do so.

A special word of thanks goes to Secretary of Housing and Urban Development Henry Cisneros, who so generously permitted the use of large portions of his 1991 speech at the American Council on Education's San Francisco meeting, some of it verbatim, as the foundation for chapter 1. I am grateful also to Donald Langenberg for the quote which opens this book and to the late Father Timothy Healy, who, before his death, granted permission for the use of his 1985 commencement address at Virginia Commonwealth University as the epilogue for this book.

I am grateful to all the urban students, faculty, and other urban colleagues whom I have had the pleasure of knowing and from whom I continue to learn so much, especially Joseph Murphy, chancellor emeritus of the City Colleges of New York, and Martin Haberman, professor of education at the University of Wisconsin—Milwaukee. Extremely important among those colleagues were LaVerne Gutsch, Kathy Lee Malone, Dottie Schmith, and Sonya Reisch, who found innumerable ways to assist and encourage me; Jean Chirila, who helped with the manuscript; and Scott Jeffress, who assisted with graphics. Additionally, Nicholas Rosselli, Tim Sutherland, and Ellen Bosman of the Indiana University Northwest library are due a special thank you for their assistance in locating resource materials. I am grateful as well to Mary Gordon in Washington, DC, for her help with reference sources.

Finally, I must express my appreciation to Indiana University President Emeritus John Ryan and the Indiana University Board of Trustees, who appointed me chancellor of Indiana University Northwest, and to the

Board of Trustees of the University of Akron, all of whom have provided me with the extraordinary opportunity of being a part of the exciting evolution of urban university education.

The Urban Campus

CHAPTER
one
❖ ❖ ❖ ❖ ❖ ❖ ❖ ❖ ❖

At the Threshold of a
New Century

The people of the United States have faced countless challenging moments in the country's relatively short history. They have forged through thickets and scaled great mountains; built highways, railroads, and bridges; witnessed the birth and death of the Industrial Age; survived the Great Depression; rejected McCarthyism; beat back Jim Crow; split the atom; and sent men to the moon. Along the way, they have also committed themselves to a system of public higher education which, despite its shortcomings, is still the envy of the world today.

THE WAY WE WERE AND THE WAY WE ARE

The commitment to public higher education was rather remarkably demonstrated at a most unlikely period in American history, during the Civil War. The nation was debating the hot issue of the abolition of slavery and the related economic issue of agricultural reform when members of the Congress in 1856 first considered a proposal to create a system of state universities. Six years later, when the very fabric of the Union was being torn by war, Congress passed the Morrill Act, setting up land-grant colleges and establishing for future generations an unparalleled access to higher education. While the concept that all citizens have the right to access was embodied in the Northwest Ordinance of 1787, Americans began to define in more specific terms, with the passage of the Morrill Act, the nature and purpose of public universities, setting out in legal language the concept that the federal government has an obligation to support higher education.

Through the passage of this historic act, Congress endowed the state land-grant colleges with 11 million acres of public land and began the process of democratizing the university system by providing for the "liberal and practical education of the industrial classes in the several pursuits and professions in life."[1] In doing so, it committed the country to investing in the raw talents and capabilities of the American people. In effect, those elected representatives of the people were saying, "We're not sure how this war is going to end, but when it does end we're going to need colleges and universities that can produce an educated citizenry to help rebuild this land." It was clear to these representatives that when the war was over there would be an enormous need for engineers who could build dams, roads, and new towns in the expanding West. They knew there would be a need for people trained in animal husbandry and in agricultural economics, and people who could build a national farm and market system. The nation's leaders also realized that teachers would be needed to make a literate populous out of the masses. So, at this very fragile moment in American history, the Congress of the United States set an important precedent by committing the country's resources to higher education.

In 1887 Congress broadened the purpose and function of the land-grant universities, passing the Hatch Act to give higher education a specific research function linked to the national goal of agricultural improvement. This goal was to be achieved through agricultural experiment stations, established with federal funds through an initial $15,000 allocation to each state. The enactment of the Morrill and Hatch acts would have far-reaching effects. Through them Congress laid the groundwork for a national network of low-cost public colleges, thus bringing higher education to people who had generally not had the opportunity to further their education, and establishing a university research relationship with the nation that has produced a bountiful harvest.

Clearly, the national investment mandated by these two pieces of legislation is one that has paid for itself many times over. It gave birth to a system of higher education that helped turn America's war-devastated fields and rural dust bowls into a productive agrarian enterprise unparalleled anywhere in the world, one that today is able to provide all the staples necessary to feed the nation, and does so with only about three percent of the labor force. Additionally, the investment helped build another unique American enterprise, our system of product distribution— the integrated process of research, production, wholesaling, transportation, and marketing that takes things from product stage and delivers them to the consumer rapidly and at a relatively low cost, sometimes even at a declining cost over time.

In the period following the passage of the Morrill and Hatch acts, access to higher education increasingly came to be defined within the context of a predominantly rural society. Before 1900 few large cities existed in the country. Partnerships between colleges and universities and their communities were forged in an agrarian economy. By the turn of the century, the nation's four largest cities had universities, but all of them were private: Columbia University in New York, the University of Chicago, Harvard University in Boston, and the University of Pennsylvania in Philadelphia. Of the 10 largest cities in the United States, however, only four had universities with enrollments in excess of two thousand.[2] In fact, only about one person in every fifteen hundred went to college.[3]

As Cleveland State University's David Sweet has pointed out, the research conducted by early agricultural experiment stations did not really begin to be transferred to the society in any significant way until after 1914, when the Smith-Lever Act linked the universities' agricultural research to the people and made the Extension Service a legal educational arm of the U.S. Department of Agriculture.[4] In the 52 years between the passage of the Morrill Act and the adoption of the Smith-Lever Act, the needs of the agrarian economy brought about a series of public policy decisions that led to the development of the first public research universities, linked to the community through extension services. Sweet points out that these linkages built the strong rural-based constituency that still provides significant lobbying support for agricultural extension programs today.

No one, of course, could have foreseen the massive change from an agrarian and industrial economy to one based on information and technology. Nor is it likely anyone could have predicted the prolific and rapid growth of American cities accompanied by dramatic demographic shifts as more and more people moved from rural to urban settings. By the 1920s, however, the trend toward urban growth was already in evidence. An article in *The Educational Record*, dated January 1923, reported, "Cities are now taking the lead in the national industry of building universities. . . . Forces are now at work behind this movement that are as irresistible as natural law."[5] In 1924, of 913 colleges reporting to the U.S. Commission of Education, 145 (15 percent) were in cities of 100,000 or more, and these enrolled more than 40 percent of all college students in the United States. Six years later, 15 of the 18 largest higher education institutions were in cities of 500,000 or more and had minimum enrollments of 10,000.[6]

With the advent of World War II and the accompanying industrialization of the American economy, a vast expansion and transformation both in the nation and in higher education began. Just as the invention of radio during World War I had given the society a giant push forward in communications, so too did World War II move the nation toward the age of information. As noted author and social theorist Peter Drucker points out in *The New Realities*, that revolutionary nudge came with the invention of the first working computer, the ENIAC, which was built for military needs with military funds.[7] Universities played an important role in the war effort, both as contributors to mobilization efforts and through their involvement with research. With the end of the war came the passage of another landmark piece of legislation that would open the doors of education even wider. The GI Bill, which made higher education accessible to veterans, was to have as great an impact on the field as did the Morrill, Hatch, and Smith-Lever acts. When veterans came home without money and unable to find jobs, they turned to higher education, which held the eventual promise of both money and jobs. Americans had always thought of opportunity as an inherent right of the individual in a free society. Now, with the closing of frontiers, the end of the war, and the passage of the GI Bill, opportunity came to be defined as educational access, and education was indelibly etched in the national conscience almost as an inalienable right.

Throughout the postwar period, college and university enrollments surged. States, seeking to meet the demand for access to higher education, began creating new types of institutions to serve rapidly growing population centers. By the 1960s, many new urban campuses and a new network of community colleges had been established throughout the United States. Indeed, by 1960 not only did all major cities have several institutions of higher education but every city with a population between 200,000 and 500,000 (there were 41) had one or more degree-granting institutions with a range of programs not only serving traditional students but also serving part-time, older, employed students.[8] Five hundred and seventy-three community colleges were established between 1955 and 1975, and, although the rate of expansion peaked in the 1960s, new growth continued, creating at least four dozen new institutions offering baccalaureate programs in urban areas during the 1980s.[9]

Last to appear on the urban scene were branches of the state and land-grant institutions, whose original rural roots ran deep. Nevertheless, by 1962 there were 150 branch campuses in urban centers, operated by 43 universities in 31 states.[10] In most states it became possible for 90 percent of the state's high school graduates to attend a public university within 25 miles of home.[11] Just as the land-grant colleges had been created in the 1860s to spur agricultural reform and to educate the "workers" of America, by the 1960s a new group of universities had emerged to meet the educational needs of the nation's burgeoning urban population.

While the creation of these new institutions was less deliberate, and although they shared no common legislative origin, their emergence can be credited in part to societal trends of the sixties that brought greater federal support for higher education. The period was characterized by well-publicized efforts to increase opportunities for people in the lower and middle socioeconomic strata and by major initiatives to end poverty and racial discrimination. The civil rights movement, the War on Poverty, and the Great Society initiatives all had far-reaching impacts both on society and on higher education. The Higher Education Act of 1965 provided one of the first general federal undergraduate scholarships (educational opportunity grants) in U.S. history. These were designed to help young people of "exceptional financial need" go to college. The legislation also introduced the work-study program as part of higher education policy. The concept of educational opportunity as an inherent right in a free society and as a means of upward mobility was again reinforced with the 1972 education bill, which added Pell Grants for needy students.

As urbanization of the nation continued, other social and political changes swept the country. Not the least of these was the women's movement. Where only a generation earlier their mothers and grandmothers were denied entry into some of the most elite university programs in the nation, women were knocking insistently at the doors of higher education and were being admitted. Even in the 1960s and 1970s many of the major professional schools had few female students and virtually no female professors, but, as University of California—Los Angeles professor Helen Astin points out, by the 1980s the effects of the social and economic changes following the women's movement were being felt throughout higher education.[12] By the end of the decade women constituted a solid 54 percent majority of all first-time, full-time students entering higher education institutions.[13] The GI Bill, the civil rights movement, the advent of federal financial aid, and the women's movement—all changed forever the face of American higher education. The era of the New Majority student had been born.

With the growth of cities and the establishment of urban colleges and universities, access also was expanded for others who had been underserved by higher education. First-generation college students from all ethnic groups and from lower-income backgrounds began graduating from urban colleges and universities in record numbers. By 1990 the nation's metropolitan populations exceeded 200 million, with rapid growth taking place in the beltways connecting cities. Prior to the emergence of the U.S. interstate highway system, urbanization had generally been characterized by the growth of a central city core and an outward, concentric expansion. However, by the 1980s there began to be rapid development of industrial and commercial activity along major transportation arteries connecting these core cities with peripheral towns and villages in such a way that it was difficult, if not impossible, to tell where one ended and the other began. This kind of growth is now frequently accompanied by the blurring of lines between two or more large population centers, such as Dallas-Fort Worth, with cities and even states stretching out to meet one another in giant urban-suburban arrangements that are coming to be known as the "megalopolis."

Whereas the United States was almost 95 percent rural at the end of the eighteenth century, today less than 25 percent of U.S. citizens live in nonurban areas (see Figure 1.1). Against this backdrop, the role of urban campuses in the society gains new significance. College access has an increasing influence on success in American society, and the intensity of the concern about access is directly related to the rapid decline in the number of good jobs available not requiring college education, accompanied by the rapid increase in the economic value of a college degree (see Figure 1.2). With changes in the economy, from an industrial base to a knowledge base, the gaps between incomes of college graduates and those with high school diplomas were much wider by the late 1980s than they had been 10 years earlier. A 1993 U.S. Bureau of Labor Statistics survey of working Americans revealed that the earnings of employed college graduates averaged $640 a week compared to $404 a week for those with only a high school diploma.[14] For white males, the payoff for a bachelor's degree was the greatest—$261 a week more than white men who do not go beyond high school. Black men with college degrees earned $236 more per week than black males with high school diplomas only.[15]

Urbanization, a different economic base, and quantum leaps in technology as well as longer life-spans and intense global competition are all changes in society that have major implications for higher education in

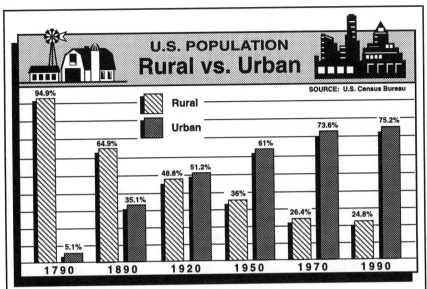

FIGURE 1.1 The population of the United States has shifted from one that was predominantly rural at the turn of the eighteenth century to one that is largely urban today.

Source: U.S. Department of Commerce, Bureau of the Census, *Number of Inhabitants, Part 1, United States Summary*, Series PC80-1, A1: 1–35. U.S. Government Printing Office, Washington, DC.

the United States. When millions of industrial jobs vanish and are replaced by jobs in service and knowledge-based industries, the need and demand for access to higher education increases. People realize that the new economy requires workers who are literate and have acquired high-level skills. The nation faces massive problems in health care, housing, infrastructure, race relations, and crime, while at the same time, the dream of higher education is now threatened by diminished resources and a decreasing federal commitment to higher education. The federal government's share of total college costs peaked in 1979, decreased in the early eighties and by 1985 accounted for just one-tenth of the costs of public higher education.[16] Meanwhile, the number of people with college degrees or advanced vocational and technical training is not likely to be nearly as great as will be needed to fill the more than two million new managerial, administrative, and technical jobs that are being created each year.[17]

As the nation faces these challenges, it does so with the knowledge that since the 1920s the prosperity of this country has generally been unmatched in the world. The gross national product and every other eco-

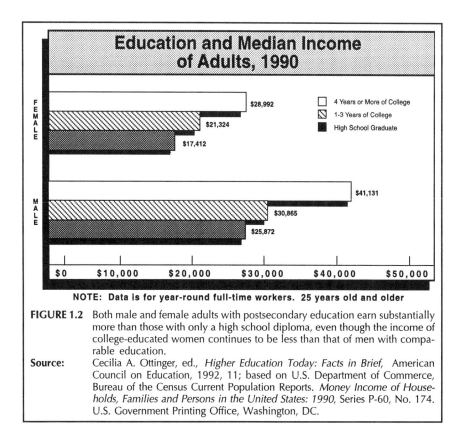

NOTE: Data is for year-round full-time workers. 25 years old and older

FIGURE 1.2   Both male and female adults with postsecondary education earn substantially more than those with only a high school diploma, even though the income of college-educated women continues to be less than that of men with comparable education.

Source: Cecilia A. Ottinger, ed., *Higher Education Today: Facts in Brief,* American Council on Education, 1992, 11; based on U.S. Department of Commerce, Bureau of the Census Current Population Reports. *Money Income of Households, Families and Persons in the United States: 1990,* Series P-60, No. 174. U.S. Government Printing Office, Washington, DC.

nomic indicator confirm that the United States has been the wealthiest nation in the world. Moreover, since the end of World War II, it also has been the leader of the free world in competition with the Soviet Communist block. Now, with the unraveling of the Soviet Union and the withdrawal of that system of centralized socialist planning from a position of world power, the stability and economic strength of the United States are vital concerns, not simply within U.S. borders but globally as well. There is no doubt that the twentieth century has been the American century.

The question is, will the United States continue to be a major world leader? The answer depends, in large measure, on the extent to which we are able to educate large portions of the society properly. Certainly, any attempt to improve conditions that exist in the country must take into account a variety of issues, including geographic differences, intergenerational divisions, race and ethnic concerns, and the widening gap between the "haves" and the "have nots," the educated and the uneducated. There can be no doubt that education, at every level and from cradle to grave, will be a major factor in what kind of nation the United States will be in the century ahead.

TWO MODELS OF DEVELOPMENT

As these issues are considered, there emerges a picture of forces that are coming together in such a way as to form two models of the society, two paradigms or frameworks within which America is developing. A clear understanding of these paradigms is vital to any interpretation of the role that urban colleges and universities must play if the nation is to remain strong and prosperous. The first paradigm is one of technology and economics, and it is comprised of a whole set of forces that work together to create the engine that pulls our nation. The second is a paradigm of demographics, of people. In many ways the two paradigms are at odds with each other, creating major challenges for higher education and for other areas of the society as well.

Consider first the framework of technology and economics. This paradigm of societal organization is characterized in three ways: (1) by the speed of communications, the rapid exchange of new knowledge and ideas; (2) by global interconnectedness, a new way of nation-states relating to each other as trading states; and (3) by the speed and ease of transportation, the ability to move people, and products, from one part of a country to another in a matter of a few hours. All of these forces create a kind of homogeneity of American life, so that the suburbs of Tampa are not really all that different from the suburbs of Sacramento. People are able to move freely throughout the country, to communicate cross-country by computer, to witness a morning news broadcast in New York and catch the evening news that same night in Atlanta, Chicago, or Los Angeles. People live for years in different places, change careers four, five, even six or more times. The "rootedness" of the past, with people growing up together in the same neighborhoods, going to the same schools and churches, and living in the same community, even the same house, for a lifetime, is disappearing.

The central force in this paradigm is technology. Often the society is more driven by the instruments at its disposal than by any kind of end objective. Quality is an absolute premium. You can walk onto the fortieth floor of almost any office building in San Francisco, Atlanta, or New York and find people who focus on new kinds of complex services that require advanced thinking, abstract thinking, critical judgment, and the ability to communicate quickly and clearly. They work in an environment where the margin for error is very slight indeed and mistakes are costly. To compete in such an environment today men and women must be educated, focused, highly skilled, and the best at what they do.

The promise of this paradigm is the real potential for people to do well, providing they are highly competent and adequately prepared for the large number of well-paying jobs that the information economy is producing. As social theorists John Naisbitt and Patricia Aburdene, authors of the book *Megatrends 2000*, state:

> The problem is how to educate and train people to qualify for an abundance of good jobs. . . . It will require a tremendous human resource effort to transform corporate America into the decentralized, customer-oriented model of the information society. Yet that is what is needed for the United States to participate fully in the booming global economy. With new markets, with a single-market Europe, and with new competitors from Asian countries, corporations need people who can think critically, plan strategically, and adapt to change.[18]

This new society is increasingly entrepreneurial in its behavior, quick, flexible, decisive, decentralized, and less tolerant of the bureaucratic behavior of large organizations that have multiple layers of management. More emphasis is placed on people deciding things in practical ways and in a decentralized fashion. Even large organizations are forming smaller units to do really important jobs. The priority is on proficiency, skill, and technological literacy. Individuals who are respected are those who are disciplined and organized, focused and efficient. As Drucker puts it, the knowledge-based society "can afford neither the schooled barbarian who makes a good living but has no life worth living, nor the cultured amateur who lacks commitment and effectiveness."[19]

Obviously, this paradigm has immense implications for the preparation of the nation's citizens and for the role urban colleges and universities must play in nurturing talent and transferring knowledge. People will need to be schooled in technology more than ever before, then re-schooled each time the technology changes. Students will need to gain a view of the rest of the world through the study of languages, histories, and cultures. They will need to learn how to learn and how to acquire continually a flexible knowledge base. Four years of college in late adolescence may have been an adequate standard in the past 50 years, but it will not be nearly enough for the century to come. The country must be committed to lifelong education, and universities must instill a kind of restless energy and excitement about learning that encourages continual self-improvement and self-education. Because of their proximity to the population, urban campuses have a particularly vital role to play.

The new societal paradigm values brain more than brawn, education and competence more than a strong back and muscle power. It is competitive, aggressive, and unforgiving. It puts social questions on the back burner and treats them as irrelevant en route to dealing with the competitive environment. It is abstract, complex, and very skilled. Only the best survive. This paradigm is the pulling end—the engine—of the national economy. It is the context into which our colleges and universities will send their students. Some will prosper; others will not. Some will be leaders; others will be left behind. This model is tremendously important, and it is the same model which is pulling the Japanese economy, the German economy, and all of the economies of the other trading states that are emerging in the global marketplace. It is the paradigm with which we must compete in order to survive. The challenge is to prepare to participate in this new technological model of society by making higher and continuing education accessible to large portions of the society where they live throughout their lives.

The second paradigm is related to people and to the dramatic demographic changes that are taking place in the country. Among these is the rapid aging of American society. By the year 2000, people in their 65th year will outnumber teens by one-third.[20] Of the 65 and older group, the number older than 85 will nearly double by the end of this century, reflecting the improving life expectancy of the population.[21] Whereas in the last century the average American male spent about 3 percent of his adult life in retirement, in this century the average American male or female could spend as much as 30 percent of his or her adult life in retirement. At the same time, people also are having fewer children, the result being that the ratio of young to old is changing. If present trends continue, instead of 4.0 people working for every person in retirement, by the early part of the next century the ratio could be 2.5 people working for every person in retirement. In fact, in their book *The New American Boom*, the writers of the Kiplinger Washington Letter tell us that by the year 2000 retirees will account for about 13 percent of the population and by 2010 the number of people older than 65 will nearly double.[22] This phenomenon has significant implications for higher education. For one thing, it is predicted that fewer young people will be entering the work force. At the same time, resources are shrinking and societal needs are growing. As the availability of educated and skilled workers becomes an increasing concern, retirees who have upgraded their education and skills are likely to be recruited to help meet predicted shortfalls in human resources. Others, facing 20 years or more of retirement, will turn to nearby colleges and universities, not simply to upgrade their education for reemployment opportunities, but also to explore new areas of learning for purposes of self-fulfillment.

The graying of America raises other concerns as well. With nearly one-third of all working adults already responsible for providing some care for an elderly person, care of the elderly is becoming a key issue in the United States. Moreover, as campus populations reflect a growing number of older students, the issue of eldercare also becomes a concern for higher education. In the near future, the concept of campus day-care may have to be broadened to include not just children but adults as well. Additionally, the aging of American society has serious financial implications. While it certainly has cost-implications in terms of health care, Social Security, and human services, it also reflects a growing redistribution of wealth in the United States. We are told, for example, that the median per capita income of elderly people has doubled since 1960, and, although the elderly constitute one-sixth of the population, America's senior citizens own one-third of all household net worth and 40 percent of all financial assets.[23] Among the challenges urban colleges and universities face is the involvement of senior citizens in higher education at every level—as students, as adjunct faculty, as paid and volunteer staff, and as supporters of post-secondary education in the best interest of the nation and of the communities in which they live.

On the other side of the demographic paradigm is the reality of a youthful population that will be quite different. The United States ended the decade of the eighties with its population growth rate at an all-time low, and even though there are more women in the prime childbearing ages of 20 to 29, the rate of childbearing continues at about 1.8 births per woman (contrasted with nearly 3.7 births per woman in the 1950s).[24] While this overall downward trend in birthrates has continued over the past 20 years, it does not hold true among minority groups, which are experiencing a growth rate two to 14 times greater than those for the nonminority population. This demographic phenomenon is largely a reflection of the youthful age structure of minority populations, which have a larger proportion of women of childbearing age. Moreover, some groups, among them Hispanics, also exhibit a higher fertility rate (almost double that of Caucasians). Additionally, the growth of some minority groups, particularly Hispanics and Asians, also is fueled by immigration. Between 1970 and 1980, for example, the Asian population grew by 142 percent, while the Hispanic population grew by approximately 61 percent. Many of these new immigrants, along with other growing minority communities, are clustered primarily in major urban areas such as Chicago, Los Angeles, and Miami.[25]

What this means for higher education is that the New Majority population on urban campuses will continue to grow (see Figure 1.3). Increasingly, institutions of higher education will draw their enrollments from the immediate urban-suburban populations around them. With a shrinking pool of traditional Caucasian college-age students, greater numbers of young Hispanics and African Americans, and an influx of older people returning to school, future urban campuses are likely to make the diversity of today's urban campuses pale in comparison.

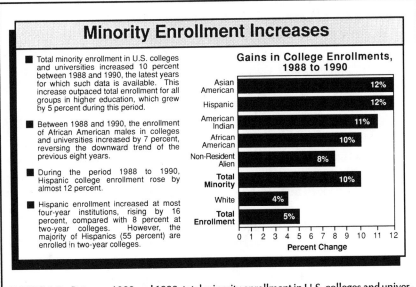

FIGURE 1.3   Between 1988 and 1990, total minority enrollment in U.S. colleges and universities increased 10 percent. This increase was greater than that of other groups. Total enrollment for all groups in higher education grew by 5 percent during this period.

Source: Cecilia A. Ottinger, ed., *Higher Education Today: Facts in Brief*, American Council on Education, February 1992, 36; based on the *Tenth Annual Report on Minorities in Higher Education*, coauthored by Deborah Carter and Reginald Wilson for the American Council on Education.

In a sense, each generation has had its own "New Majority." After World War II, the new majority was veterans; in the sixties and seventies it was African Americans and women. At the end of the Vietnam War it was Asians. Traditionally, U.S. cities have been the staging areas for the first step on the ladder of integration into American society. Today the staging areas include urban campuses. But in comparison, the urbanization trend we are seeing in the 1990s is unprecedented in the nation's history. California offers a prime example. With about 30 million people in the latest census, California has a greater population than any other state.[26] The state with the next largest population is New York, with approximately 17 million people. A study of the state of California tells us that by the year 2000 its white and Hispanic populations will be about equal, each with about 42 percent.[27] San Francisco will be 65 percent minority. Los Angeles County, with about 8 million people, will be 60 percent Hispanic, Asian, and black. These new demographics, in varying degrees, are being reflected in states all across the country and will have a major impact on the U.S. work force. From 1988 to 2000, for example, it is estimated that Hispanics will add more than 5 million workers to the labor force, accounting for 27 percent of the net change. The number of women will rise by 22 percent, blacks by 24.4 percent, and Asians by 53.4 percent.[28] All of higher education will feel the impact of this new population mix, but urban campuses will experience it most intensely. It is important to note, too, that change is a constant. In the twenty-first century, the expansion of these demographic shifts will be almost limitless.

Another challenging dimension of these demographic changes will be related to economics. Although it still may be argued that the United States is better off financially than it was 20 years ago, the nation still struggles with the intractable problem of poverty (see Figure 1.4). In 1992, 36.9 million Americans, 14.5 percent of the population, lived below the poverty line. While the number of individuals living in poverty has decreased, falling from a high of 38.6 million in 1962, far too many children are growing up in poor families, many of them in single-parent households.[29] In 1992 the poverty rate for children under 18 was 21.9 percent; for blacks it was 33.3 percent; and for Hispanics it was 29.3 percent.[30] Many of those living below the poverty line are working poor, most of them uneducated or undereducated, employed in minimum-wage jobs, and living in cities. The cost of poverty to society in general is astronomical, as is evidenced in higher taxes to support social services, money required to provide health care for the indigent, for unemployment

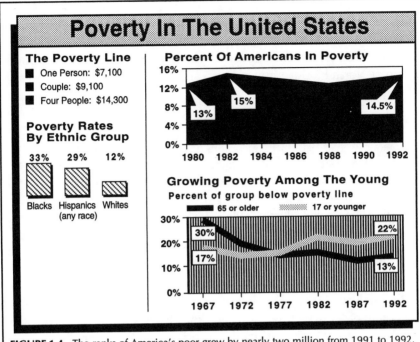

FIGURE 1.4 The ranks of America's poor grew by nearly two million from 1991 to 1992, bringing the level of poverty in the population to 14.5 percent. Almost 22 percent of children under 18 were living below the poverty line.

Source: Adapted from a Knight-Ridder/Media Tribune Services graphic illustration, "Poverty in a Rich Nation," *Post-Tribune*, 5 October 1993, A:3. Reprinted by permission: Knight-Ridder Tribune Graphics Service.

compensation and penal institutions, to say nothing of street crime, homelessness, domestic violence, child neglect, and the underground drug culture.

The rate of poverty can be reduced to the extent that people can be empowered through education to become productive participants in society. Education will increasingly control access to jobs. As America continues to change, the disparity between the paradigm of the competitive, technology-driven society and the paradigm of people becomes more obvious. The match is not a very good one.

HIGHER EDUCATION FOR A CHANGING SOCIETY

In considering urban colleges and universities within the context of a society very different from just a few years ago, it is useful to consider the two paradigms because of the economic and demographic realities that must be reckoned with as our institutions of higher education look to the future. It is useful, too, to consider some of these trends in the broader context of cities and their suburbs, which are inextricably linked. John Bardo of North Florida University, in an article discussing this issue, says:

> The term "urban university" has generally implied a central city focus with an emphasis on access, job-related professional education, and applied research in addition to basic research. Yet the need for educational assistance transcends this limited focus and circum-scribed political boundary. Suburban minorities (more than ten million people) require access; poverty in the suburbs is still a travesty; suburban and satellite city blight is as persistent as any in a central city, and employers on the periphery require trained person-nel as much as do those who are more centrally located. We may be much better served if we recast these issues as human problems of our urban society than the unique problem of a particular political jurisdiction.[31]

In *The New Realities* Drucker describes the advent of a new social and economic order, which he calls the "knowledge society." It is character-ized by a pluralist organization of institutions, a transnational economy, a rapidly changing information base, and, above all, a continuing need for education.[32] In this society, Drucker says, all members must be literate, not only in reading, writing, and mathematics, but also in computer skills and technology and in understanding a world in which boundaries of town, nation, and country do not define or limit an individual's horizon.[33] In such a society, engineers, physicians, attorneys, educators, computer pro-grammers, and geologists are all obsolete within a few years if they have not refreshed their knowledge at periodic intervals. Meeting the needs of urban America, within the context and challenges of this new society, will not be easy. It will require an investment of time, tireless effort, financial resources, and expanded opportunities for education. One of the great promises of a knowledge-based society, however, is its potential to create a better life for many people. It is very clear that urban colleges and universities have a unique and critical role to play in the revitalization of the United States. Just as higher education made the difference in agrarian America during the Civil War, one of the gravest moments in U.S. history, so today our urban institutions are called upon to assume a similar role. What worked in the past will not work for the future.

Teachers and administrators in urban higher education have an oppor-tunity to touch human lives now and in the decades to come. The late professor, Ross Toole, historian at the University of Montana, gave some advice worth pondering. He said:

> My generation has made America the most affluent country on earth. It has tackled head-on a racial problem, which no nation in the history of mankind has dared to do. It has publicly declared war on poverty, and it has gone to the moon. It has desegregated schools and abolished polio. It has presided over the beginning of the greatest social and economic revolution in history. It has declared itself and committed itself and taxed itself in the cause of social justice and reform. It has begun these things, not finished them.[34]

The reality is that many of the goals he was talking about are never fully reached, but if America is going to be strong as it has been through this century, then the job of improving it will fall in no small measure on the urban colleges and universities, because it is they who must educate the largest and most diverse numbers of its citizens. In the same way that the land-grant institutions rose to the task of serving rural America, so too must the "asphalt aggies" of contemporary higher education serve our urban society in these critical times and in the decades to come.

REFERENCES

The impetus for and development of this chapter were drawn from a 1991 speech delivered at the annual meeting of the American Council on Education by urban scholar and former San Antonio Mayor Henry Cisneros, who is now U.S. Secretary for Housing and Urban Development. Large portions of the speech, particularly those relating to societal paradigms and demographic changes in the country, are used in their entirety. The author gratefully acknowledges these substantive contributions of Dr. Cisneros and his generous permission to use these materials. His insight into the challenges facing society and his perceptions of the role urban higher education must play as the U.S. enters the twenty-first century are reflected not only in this chapter but throughout the book.

1. U.S. Department of Health, Education and Welfare, *Land GrantColleges and Universities 1862–1962* (Washington, DC: GPO, 1962), 3.
2. J. Martin Klotsche, *The Urban University: And the Future of Our Cities* (New York: Harper & Row, 1966), 4–5.
3. David C. Sweet, "Urban Extension in the Decade Ahead: Collaboration, Competition, or Contraction" (paper presented at the North

Central States Cooperative Extension Service Urban Conference, Chicago, Illinois, 18 April 1991), 5.

4. Ibid.

5. S. P. Capen, "Program for Progress in Education," *The Educational Record* (January 1923): 6–7.

6. Klotsche, *The Urban University*, 4–5.

7. Peter F. Drucker, *The New Realities* (New York: Harper & Row, 1989), 48.

8. Klotsche, *The Urban University*, 4–5.

9. Charles E. Hathaway, Paige E. Mulhollan, and Karen A. White, "Metropolitan Universities—Models for the Twenty-First Century," *Metropolitan Universities* 1 (Spring 1990): 10–11.

10. C. K. Arnold, "Community Campuses of State Universities," *Saturday Review* (1 March 1962): 92.

11. Helen S. Astin, "Educating Women: A Promise and a Vision for the Future," *American Journal of Education* (August 1990): 480–81. First published by the University of Chicago, 1990.

12. Ibid.

13. Ibid.

14. Dottie Enrico (*Newsday*), "White Men Get Best College Payoff," *Indiana Daily Student*, 6 October 1993, 5.

15. Ibid.

16. Gary Orfield, "Public Policy and College Opportunity," *American Journal of Education* (August 1990): 323–26. First published by the University of Chicago, 1990.

17. John Naisbitt and Patricia Aburdene, *Megatrends 2000: Ten New Directions for the 1990s* (New York: Avon Books, 1990; reprint, New York: William Morrow, 1990), 34 (page citations are to Avon edition).

18. Ibid.

19. Drucker, *The New Realities*, 245.

20. The Staff of the Washington Letter, *The New American Boom* (Washington, DC: Kiplinger Washington Editors, 1986), 22.

21. *The New American Boom*, 23.

22. Ibid.

23. Naisbitt and Aburdene, *Megatrends 2000*, 31.

24. Leobardo F. Estrada, "Anticipating the Demographic Future," *Change* (May/June 1989): 14–19.

25. Ibid.

26. *The New American Boom*, 63.

27. Ibid.

28. U.S. Department of Labor, Bureau of Labor Statistics, "Outlook 2000: The Labor Force," *Occupational Outlook Quarterly* 33 (Fall 1989): 6–7.
29. Sonya Ross (Associated Press), "Poverty Rate at All-Time High," *Indiana Daily Student*, 5 October 1993, 6.
30. Ibid.
31. John W. Bardo, "University and City from Urban to Metropolitan," *Metropolitan Universities* 1 (Spring 1990): 38–41.
32. Drucker, *The New Realities*, 233–52.
33. Ibid.
34. Ross Toole, *An Angry Man Talks Up to Youth* (New York: Award Books, 1970), 13.

CHAPTER
two
✦ ✦ ✦ ✦ ✦ ✦ ✦ ✦ ✦

Urban Campuses:
The Critical Connection

Any discussion of urban higher education must begin with an attempt to define urban campuses—how they have come to be, how they are distinct from traditional schools of higher education, and how they are perceived both by the general public and within the academy. In making this kind of analysis, however, we need to remember that for evolving institutions such as urban campuses the process of becoming is not yet finished. More importantly, the task they are performing cannot wait until we have agreed upon a definition or have assigned these institutions to a category in the taxonomy of higher education.

In reality, a higher education monolith probably never existed, but if one did exist, it has long since passed from the scene. Even among the most homogeneous schools of any period one can observe major differences in emphasis, philosophy, and organization, and despite the deliberate speed of the academy, new forms of educational delivery are continually emerging. Predictably, and sometimes fortunately, the old forms are rarely eliminated, at least not completely. More often new forms are tailored out of the old by changing realities. And while critics frequently argue that American higher education is bound by tradition to such an extent that it is generally unresponsive even to radically changing needs, those inside the academy understand that the collective whole of the enterprise is constantly shifting, changing, and evolving.

University of Maryland Chancellor Langenberg points out that the changing nature of the academy is not the only reason it is difficult to articulate a definition. Another difficulty involves the variance in perception between those inside the academy and the university's patrons and clients in the larger community. Says Langenberg:

One might think that an institution that originated near the beginning of the millennium now nearing its end would long ago have settled the question of what it is for. Not so. We find ourselves today in the midst of vigorous debate about the fundamental purposes and functions of the university. . . . Such debate within the academy is not unusual; it is endemic. . . . What is notable about the current debate is the extent to which it is occurring outside the academy. . . . Nearly everybody seems to know what universities should be providing them, and to doubt that universities are doing so. On one thing, though, there is widespread agreement. It is that universities can no longer set themselves apart from the mainstream of human events, from the central issues of the day.[1]

Given the fluidity and variety of institutional models, we might ask, Why bother with definitions at all? The answer may be that, practically speaking, they are useful to those outside the academy who need a system in order to sort out the complexity of the more than 3,000 institutions of higher education in the United States. As a result of this demand, a taxonomy of sorts exists among institutions. Governmental agencies, legislative groups, accrediting bodies, foundations, and others rely on the categories as a means of interacting with a wide variety of institutions in global, though it could be argued not always sensible, ways. Certainly, it is doubtful that anyone could demonstrate that any of the widely accepted categories are precise. That Michigan State University and the University of Kentucky are both known as land-grant institutions simply means they share some important origins, values, and missions. No one could argue, however, that because they are both labeled "land grant," the two are replicas of one another.

Still, definitive categories do exert significant influence. Moreover, as new models of higher education emerge they are often seriously disadvantaged by the lack of recognition and understanding of their presence and role. In due time, of course, history, the existence of national boards, and the nature of discourse in the academy guarantee each new kind of university will receive a title. Once this is accomplished, the university category will be embraced by all and granted some acceptance in the fold. In the interim, however, the significance of emerging kinds of campuses is very real and a discussion of them is warranted. Such is the current situation of urban colleges and universities, which, although called by many names, are not generally categorically defined. One needs only to recognize how many higher education students in the United States are attending urban colleges and universities to know that description, definition, and recognition not only are called for but are probably long overdue.

Even the Carnegie Foundation taxonomy provides no appropriate niche for those colleges and universities that both exist in and take special measures to serve metropolitan populations. The closest definition is in the comprehensive universities category, which is defined as campuses that offer baccalaureate education and some graduate education through the master's degree, with more than half of their baccalaureate degrees awarded in one or more occupational or professional areas. But this category says nothing about delivery, philosophy, or mission, all of which are generally quite important to any definition of urban institutions. Moreover, many urban campuses grant doctoral degrees and therefore would be placed in Carnegie's doctorate-granting universities category. Some are two-year colleges and so would fall under that heading. Because of their extensive research efforts, other urban campuses would be placed in the research university category. Additionally, the numbers of students enrolled—also a consideration in the Carnegie taxonomy—varies widely among urban institutions. Moreover, other popular college and university classifications, such as the yearly ranking by *U.S. News and World Report*, also provide no appropriate definition for or recognition of urban institutions as a special group of campuses with increasing significance.

WHAT IS AN URBAN CAMPUS?

If it is generally difficult to define "the university," as Langenberg points out, it certainly is even more challenging to define urban colleges and universities. The commitment of those institutions to be engaged with people in the communities they serve, however, is at least one major and commonly accepted descriptor. At its simplest level, the term urban university refers to an institution of higher education located in a city, but there is almost universal agreement that not all universities situated in or near cities can be defined in an urban context. Even the fact that a university located in a city is actively engaged with those in its community does not give it an urban identity. No one, for example, would be likely to define Yale University in an urban context, although, over the past several years, it has invested heavily in the city of New Haven and is a significant partner in the city's downtown renewal and economic development efforts.

Neither does student population alone define the urban campus. Certainly, universities in metropolitan areas are likely to serve far more commuters, part-timers, minorities, women, and older students than are their sister institutions in nonurban locations, but while student diversity is a major descriptor, it only contributes to a full definition of the institution. Academic programs and degrees awarded do not play a distinctive role in definition either. The highest degree offered by Miami-Dade Community College, with more than 50,000 students, is at the associate degree level, while the highest offered at the University of Texas at San Antonio, with approximately 14,000 students, is at the doctorate level. Both are undeniably urban institutions.

The age of urban campuses does not seem to be a definitive factor either. The University of Louisville and Wichita State University—both urban campuses—have origins dating back to the 1800s. The University of Akron dates back to 1870, while the University of North Carolina at Charlotte was established in 1960. Likewise, no common origins exist among urban institutions. Some began as private colleges with religious affiliations, some as community colleges operated with local funds, and some as branch campuses of land-grant institutions.

If not solely by location, involvement with the community, student population, academic programs, age, or origin, how then can we define those colleges and universities that are emerging as primary institutions for the delivery of higher education to the majority of U.S. citizens today? I would suggest at this point that a definition must be based on philosophy, by the way the institution sees itself in relation to its environment and to the community in which it is located. Urban colleges and universities are part and parcel of the metropolitan milieu. They are not simply in or near the city; they are *of* the city. As University of Illinois—Chicago professor Anthony Orum puts it, "Cities are made; they are not natural. They also are fascinating because of the social and human forces that universally animate them."[2] The urban campus is chief among those forces, but the relationship between city and university is symbiotic. Each feeds the other's hunger and each fills the other's need. As Indiana University professor George Kuh and coauthors of *Involving Colleges* point out, the level of city-university interaction varies. "The critical factor for using the urban setting to educational advantage," say the authors, "is the extent to which the institution and its agents—faculty members, administrators, and staff, have accepted and are enthusiastically pursuing the institution's mission as an urban or metropolitan university."[3]

Cleveland State University's President Emeritus Walter Waetjen and CSU's former director of institutional research John Muffo view urban institutions in the context of a continuum.[4] At one end is the traditional university that just happens to be located in the city. At the other is the institution that is outwardly oriented. The traditional institution, although it is surrounded by problems that confront the urban milieu, makes no pretense of trying to solve the dilemmas and has no intercourse with the city, except perhaps through intercollegiate athletics and performing arts activities. The institution that is outwardly oriented is distinguished by its efforts to realize urban mission objectives. It involves its students and faculty in direct services to the community—health care clinics, economic development initiatives, area-specific research, legal services, and housing and environmental studies, to name a few—and to some degree becomes a research and social service university. Between the two extremes is the urban institution that Waetjen and Muffo describe as "transitional," the college or university that has struggled to identify reasonable ways in which its urban location and opportunities can be integrated with traditional values and operations of academe. "If some institutions have been successful in identifying ways in which their urban mission goals could be realized," the authors assert, "it is safe to say that many have not—despite valiant efforts."[5] Waetjen and Muffo, like many others, argue in favor of an urban model based on that of the land-grant universities, with modifications that would allow for a broader, cross-disciplinary approach.

While it may be useful to examine the extension service aspect of the land-grant model, and perhaps even to adapt it in some instances, the mission of the land-grant institutions was more narrowly focused when compared to that of urban universities. Wright State University's President Emeritus Paige Mulhollan, University of Arkansas—Little Rock chancellor Charles Hathaway, and University of Nebraska—Omaha dean of fine arts Karen White argue that in establishing interactions with the metropolitan environment we need to think creatively about the ways we might use the entire body of the university as an urban-based experimental station.[6] As the urban university evolves, no doubt many variations of the model will emerge. Indeed, as Mulhollan, Hathaway, and White insisted in a 1990 article, when all three were colleagues at Wright State, "there can be no single interpretation of the model for a metropolitan university."[7]

TERMS FOR URBAN CAMPUSES

Other terms are also useful in describing universities serving today's large population centers. Some members of the academic arena favor the words "urban college or university" as the most encompassing term; others prefer "metropolitan university," believing that it has a broader connotation; and a few would choose the words "city college or university." A variety of other phrases have been used, including "hyphenated campuses," "campuses in a context," and "asphalt aggies." Nearly all of these have a historical frame of reference.

As a matter of fact, "city" was the first word used to describe campuses in large population areas. The term could mean any one of a number of things. The campus may have been designated as an institution that served only those who lived in the city, as it did with the City University of New York (CUNY) and City Colleges of Chicago. In other instances a distinguished private institution, such as the University of Chicago, may simply have decided to honor the city in which it was located by using its name.

The city colleges and universities were certainly the historic forebearers of today's urban universities. CUNY, for example, was founded in 1847 as the City College of New York, and although CUNY's mission from the beginning was to serve the poor, the disadvantaged, and the sons and daughters of New York City's working class, the earliest use of the term "city" generally was an indicator of location rather than institutional mission. Some institutions designated as "city" came into being as an integral part of the city. The University of Louisville, for example, was chartered as a municipal institution in 1798 when the city was just 20 years old, and the history of the university and its hometown are almost inseparable. Today, even though the University of Louisville is now the state's premier urban institution of higher education, its municipal heritage is still highly prized, and its ties to the city remain strong.

It wasn't until much later—after World War II—that the term "urban" came into use, again primarily to designate universities and colleges that happened to be located in cities. Some of these campuses, like the University of Tennessee at Chattanooga, established in 1886 as a normal school, became urban as the city grew up around them and they changed to a public affiliation. Others designated as urban were deliberately established in heavily populated areas for the dual purpose of serving a major population center and because they could benefit by being in close proximity to other institutions of the city, that is, hospitals, schools, museums and theaters, businesses, and industry. Because of their location near the work force, many of these institutions came to enroll a great many older, part-time, and financially independent students. In most cases, however, they were not established for the avowed purpose of attracting independent students. Nevertheless, as a result of their changing enrollment profile, some of the first national collective efforts of these public urban campuses were associated with the drive for financial aid and special support services for adults who were not well prepared for college. While some of these campuses constructed residence halls, others came to be known as urban commuter institutions, because most of their students were older, part-time, and living off-campus. Additionally, many urban campuses established fine track records in recruiting and serving minority students. Both Indiana University Northwest and the University of Missouri, Saint Louis, are examples of excellent universities that are defined and have distinguished themselves as "urban."

A more recent designation for these city-based colleges and universities is the term "metropolitan." Although institutions that use this designation are located in or on the outskirts of large cities, they sometimes view themselves as distinct from the "city" and "urban" institutions for one or more reasons: they (1) may or may not use the city name or have city support; (2) may or may not serve student populations that are largely part-time, adult, or minority; (3) often have large residential student bodies; and (4) sometimes are located on the periphery of the city or even some miles away in a suburban setting. Despite these distinctions, the focus in research and service opportunities of these universities is purposefully and closely linked to the city, and many of their students are drawn from the area in which the campus is located. In 1990, following a national conference, nearly 50 institutions of higher education officially claimed the "metropolitan" designation, signing a formal declaration about their nature and goals. Among those represented in this category are institutions with such varied origins and characteristics as George Mason University in Fairfax, Virginia; Memphis State University in Tennessee; the University of Central Florida in Orlando; and the University of Colorado at Denver.

The lines of distinction between the designations of city, urban, and metropolitan are quite blurred. Some of those who have claimed the definition of "metropolitan," for example, the University of Louisville and Wichita State, have deep roots in the city and an external identity that would likely be described as urban. As Ernest Lynton, executive editor of the *Metropolitan Universities* journal, has pointed out, however, the use of the words "metropolitan universities" is purposefully plural. Says Lynton:

> There exists no single model for the metropolitan university, no uniquely defined set of programs and activities, no blueprint for the ideal organization and mode of operation. Among the several hundred institutions that fall into this broad rubric, both in this country and abroad, one finds not only a great variety in detail, but differences as well with regard to some basic issues, if not in kind then in degree. Few would cavil at the statement that metropolitan universities have a special obligation toward the population of their region, but there exists a range of views as to the degree of this relationship. Broad consensus exists, as well, about the need for metropolitan universities to pay attention to the dissemination and application of new knowledge and to contribute to the economic and cultural development of their area. But on this issue as well one finds differences of opinion as to the degree of emphasis, and a wide variety in the proposed manner of implementation.[8]

Several other terms are used in connection with urban colleges and universities, some of them less seriously than others. One of the more interesting, though not particularly definitive, is the term "hyphenated university," a label that is said to have emanated from the frustration of a well-known coach whose championship team fell to a team he viewed as an upstart urban competitor. Lamenting that "these hyphenated campuses all seem to be on a mission from God," the coach recognized the energy and toughness of his competitor and coined a phrase that is still used from time to time in the lexicon of urban academe. While the label leaves something to be desired, it does make a point. While most colleges and universities must develop standards, traditions, and indexes of excellence over long periods of time, many of the "hyphenated campuses" came into being with assumptions of quality and reputation already in place. The University of Illinois—Chicago, for example, started out with standards of excellence that had evolved through a university system with more than a century of service. Although the term "hyphenated university" may be frivolous, the real significance of the designation is found in the unique combination of the traditions of an older, established campus with the energy of an emerging one. The two have complementary strengths which together make the whole of the university far more than the sum of its parts. Additionally, it is interesting that while not all "hyphenated campuses" are located in large population areas—and therefore not all are urban—most of them are in cities.

Many of the terms used to designate urban colleges and universities are, in fact, acknowledgments of the specific context that is part of the institution's identity. For example, the name "University of Maryland—Baltimore County" says, "We are the University of Maryland operating in support of and in cooperation with a context that is Baltimore County." The name of the University of Arkansas—Little Rock provides students and the public with the same message. The context in which service is rendered becomes an integral part of the institutional identity. Communicating identity by means of adjoining the geographical area involved with the institution has precedent in the land-grant universities, which almost always adopted the name of the state they served.

When the coach tagged his urban competitor with the name "hyphenated university," he was, in fact, describing the campus in a particular context, which happened to be its alliance with a specific university. Urban institutions as a group tend to share certain contextual points of reference. For example, the context of the student has a direct bearing on how these campuses engage their energies and organize themselves. They schedule classes to accommodate older working, commuting, and part-time students who generally have needs very different from full-time, residential students. As a result, most urban campuses teach from early morning until late into the evening, and full class schedules are the norm year-round. Additionally, many of these institutions have a nonrestrictive approach to admissions, acknowledging that the students they serve are likely to be more diverse and that each student will arrive in his or her own context, with a unique and special set of needs. That they tend to have less restrictive admissions standards, however, does not mean that most of the institutions in this group have open admissions policies. While some colleges identified as urban do open their doors to anyone who wants to enroll, others have quite stringent admission requirements. What is meant by nonrestrictive is that these institutions do not usually limit themselves to a monolithic student body. As a result they generally serve a wide range of ages, persons both married and unmarried, students from a vast array of ethnic and economic backgrounds, and those with varied academic goals and purposes for attending. Increasingly, they are serving postbaccalaureate students who are upgrading and acquiring new skills.

Another label sometimes used for urban campuses is the "interactive university." Those institutions embracing this designation tend to find more ways of interfacing and interacting with off-campus realities than do those more traditionally modeled. It is far too tidy, as well as inaccurate, to suggest that such involvement is always the direct result of a well-defined mission, though in some cases, as with the University of Louisville, this is true. Most urban campuses have reached out to the city for multiple reasons—some simply because of proximity, others because it was in their own self-interest, others because they felt a responsibility to their communities, and others just because it seemed a thing to do. While an ivory tower isolationist stance may come easy in a rural or small-town setting, it is quite difficult to maintain in the bustle of metro America. When the city transit stop is located on the campus—as it is at Bunker Hill Community College in Boston—it is almost impossible for the campus to be unchanged. When campus and community breathe the same air, drink the same water, and face the same opportunities, problems, and even dangers in a shared environment, it is not reasonable for either to ignore the other.

Although the label "interactive" is not distinct to campuses in large population centers, the state of symbiotic involvement implied in the term can often more easily occur in an urban setting. For the interactive campus, involvement is generally the result of a deliberate decision. In a very real sense this decision represents an overt rejection of the traditional university value that ascribes great intellectual benefit to being aloof and apart. With an interactive model, frequently the lines are not sharply drawn between campus and research park, applied and basic research, regular credit classes and executive education, and a host of other things that in an earlier time and on traditional campuses were considered properly distinct and separate. The interactive campus sometimes even defines itself as an urban laboratory and is characterized by a clearly articulated mission to help solve urban problems—problems ranging from industrial productivity and crime prevention to enhancing the quality of life through cleaner air and better schools.

An interactive posture represents a dramatic departure from that of many traditional universities, who would even question contributions to knowledge that are developed in a setting with variables so difficult to control. Even so, while institutions with interactive goals have detractors in academe, other people praise these emerging institutions for the success and strengths of their partnerships. Allan Ostar, past president of the American Association of State Colleges and Universities, characterizes these institutions in this way:

> Interactive universities organize themselves to meet the needs of their students and communities. They emphasize the value of classroom

teaching and the relationship between professors and students in the pursuit of knowledge. They encourage and support the scholarship of their faculties; provide educational opportunity to all sectors of society; and contribute significantly to the economic and cultural development of their communities, regions and states.[9]

"Asphalt aggies," a label as frivolous as the term "hyphenated campuses," also is sometimes used to describe urban colleges and universities, but not without context and meaning. As discussed in the first chapter, America's system of low-cost public institutions grew from the great land-grant universities that were established by Congress as a means of accomplishing agricultural progress. Affectionately known as the "aggies," these fine institutions were created to forge partnerships between universities and the agrarian society for the purpose of transferring knowledge through research and teaching. County agents took the technology from laboratories and classrooms directly to U.S. farms and factories. The success of the agricultural and technical land-grant university is unparalleled in history, and, among other great contributions, land-grant universities have made America's system of agribusiness the envy of the world. Still, because the "aggies" model permitted the academy to maintain at least some degree of traditional university aloofness from the society, it was not a total interactive model. The university simply found answers through its research mechanisms and then transferred those answers to a farming public through a "middle man" operation known as the agricultural extension center.

Great agriculture schools generally maintained their own livestock and experimental farms and stations and did not rely only on working farms as their primary laboratories. Thus, although the aggies had a mission to change and improve the environment, they remained somewhat separate from the setting in which their influence was eventually felt. Similarities, however, between today's emerging institutions in urban settings and those land-grant universities can be discerned. Both models interface directly with the needs of the society, and both have the goal of educating the dominant population of the day. Today, the city is the urban laboratory, with the university transferring knowledge to many segments of the community—business, industry, schools, and hospitals, among others. As a result of these obvious parallels, the asphalt aggies is not as frivolous a label as it might seem at first.

"City," "urban," "metropolitan," "commuter," "hyphenated," "interactive," "campuses in a context," and "asphalt aggies" then are a few of the labels assigned to the colleges and universities that serve our major population centers. Any comprehensive definition of urban campuses must take into account certain shared characteristics that make these institutions uniquely identifiable as a group. Title XI of the Higher Education Act ascribes the obvious characteristics: (1) they are located in urban areas; (2) they draw a substantial portion of their undergraduate students from urban areas and from areas that are contiguous to their location; and (3) they carry out programs to make postsecondary education opportunities more accessible to residents of urban (and contiguous) areas.

DIVERSE STUDENT BODY

The Title XI description is a good start, but it does not tell the whole story. One marked characteristic of urban campuses is a highly diverse student profile, evidenced in several ways, among them variance in student goals, length of time spent on campus, matriculation patterns, and a wide variety of generational, ethnic, economic, cultural, marital, racial, and gender differences. (The nature and scope of these will be discussed in greater detail in chapter 3.) Certainly, no understanding of the nature of urban campuses can be complete without knowing something about the lives and expectations of the students enrolled. In terms of goals, students pursue a much wider range of objectives than would normally be encountered among students on traditional campuses. These range from taking one class in order to upgrade a skill or learn about a particular subject to completion of a baccalaureate degree and postgraduate study. Consequently, urban institutions generally provide multiple stepping-stone options at several degree and nondegree levels to meet differing needs. As expected life-span has lengthened and the rate of change has accelerated, the number of older students is increasing on almost every campus.

Matriculation patterns also reveal a dramatic departure from traditional campus norms. With part-time students comprising an increasing majority at urban colleges and universities, the period of degree-program study may extend from the traditional four years to as many as eight or 10 years. Many students are enrolled only in evening classes; others, because of work or family responsibilities, are restricted to weekend attendance. Often, a pattern of continuation includes "stop out" periods, times when the student temporarily leaves the university to take care of matters more pressing. Marriage, pregnancy, caring for young children or elderly parents, divorce, death in the family, added work responsibilities, military duty, and financial problems may result in "stop out," but urban students demonstrate determination and persistence toward the end goal. Within the urban matriculation profile, a traditional time frame is not assumed or even particularly valued by students (see Figure 2.1). More and more students on urban campuses understand the university as an intellectual delivery system and not just as an academic rite of passage for late adolescence. In the spring of 1993, as I shook his hand at commencement, a graduate whispered to me that it had taken him 25 years to earn his degree.

Diversity on urban campuses achieves its broadest definition, however, not in terms of student goals or matriculation patterns but in differences of background, age, culture, and ethnicity among other things (see Figure 2.1). More than half of urban campus students are older than 18 to 22 years, and many are in their thirties and forties; the majority are women; and minority representation is increasing, reflecting the nature of the urban society in which the campus is located. At Miami-Dade Community College the ethnic mix of students is about 23 percent white; 19 percent African American; 55 percent Hispanic; 2 percent Asian; and less than 1 percent Native American.[10] At Queens College in New York, 40 percent of the students are minorities and 45 percent are immigrants or

Enrollment in U.S. Colleges and Universities

	American Indian	Asian	Black	Hispanic	White	Foreign
Total	103	555	1,223	758	10,675	397
Public	90	445	952	648	8,340	265
Private	12	109	271	110	2,335	132
Men	43	287	476	344	4,841	248
Women	60	268	747	414	5,834	149
Four-year	48	343	715	344	6,757	322
Two-year	54	212	509	414	3,918	75
Undergraduate	95	485	1,124	702	9,231	226
Graduate	6	52	84	46	1,221	165
Professional	1	18	16	10	222	5

SOURCE: U.S. Department of Education

FIGURE 2.1 1990 Enrollment by Racial and Ethnic Group (in thousands). The student populations of U.S. colleges and universities reflect the growing diversity that characterizes American society. On urban campuses, diversity is most evident in cultural and ethnic differences.

Source: *Chronicle of Higher Education*, 22 January 1992, A-37; based on figures supplied by the U.S. Department of Education.

children of immigrants.[11] In the predominantly urban 20-campus California State University system, enrollment in the fall of 1990 stood at 369,000, with a demographic breakdown that looked like this: 64 percent white, 12 percent Asian, 6 percent African American, 15 percent Latino, and about 1 percent Native American.[12] Four campuses in this system have more than 30,000 students each, and on some CSU campuses the concentration of students over age 25 is greater than 70 percent.[13]

One additional characteristic of students enrolled in urban institutions is that most of them come to the campus in a context other than that of just being a student. For them, the end educational goal—whether a degree, a certificate, or simply the completion of a particular course—is not their only major objective during the time they are involved with the university. In fact, education may not even be the most important goal. These students come to the campus with a primary identity that is far less likely to be "student" than on traditional residential campuses. For example, the student might enroll in a context that includes roles as husband, father, company comptroller, weekend Army Reserve officer, volunteer fireman, church deacon, and student. Additionally, the priority of the various roles can shift as family, work, community involvement, and other responsibilities and interests change.

COMMUNITY INTERACTION

In defining those higher education institutions *of* the megalopolis, we have already touched on another characteristic that is generally essential in their philosophy and mission, their involvement with the world beyond the university itself. In the urban environment, isolation of the academic enterprise is not valued for its sake alone. Most of urban campuses are based on a collaborative model characterized by alliances and partnerships involving both public and private sectors—schools, community agencies, neighborhood organizations, professional associations, urban planning organizations, city government, health providers, the media, and others. Research-park ventures are common. The university and the arts community pool resources, both financial and human, to build museums and theaters, to sponsor exhibitions and stage productions. As an example, in Kentucky, the University of Louisville's teaching hospital treated nearly 160,000 people in 1990 alone.[14]

In some emerging urban institutions the margin between town and gown is eradicated. George Mason University president George Johnson describes it this way:

> The interactive [university] is deeply involved in the turbulence of
> the social environment. It thinks while doing. . . . When I talk about
> this kind of relationship with the community, those in higher educa-
> tion jump to the conclusion that we are a service institution and not
> a research institution—that we aren't a major university. But we're in
> a position where we have an opportunity to link those two, to do
> both.[15]

Urban campuses, through their interactive missions, fall into what
author Peter Drucker calls the "new third sector of the knowledge society,"
one he characterizes as a "counterculture of values."[16] This third sector of
nonbusiness, nongovernment, "human-change agencies," is made up of
nonprofit organizations and includes the majority of America's hospitals,
a great percentage of its colleges and universities, and large philanthropic
organizations such as the United Way, the Girl Scouts, the Urban League,
and the Salvation Army. Most of these institutions are supported primarily by fees and voluntary donations, but many also are tax-supported.
Most are operated autonomously, have their own budgets, and are run by
administrators chosen by a board. What they all have in common, however, is that their purpose is to help change human beings. For the
hospital, the product is a patient who becomes well. For the Salvation
Army it is perhaps a derelict who becomes a citizen. For the urban
university it is a local resident who, through education, is prepared to
make a living *and* a life. Says Drucker:

> America's third-sector institutions are rapidly becoming creators of
> new bonds of community and a bridge across the widening gap
> between knowledge workers and the "other half." Increasingly they
> create a sphere of effective citizenship. One hears a good deal these
> days about the disintegrations of community; the family, for in-
> stance. . . . But in the third-sector institution new bonds of community
> are being formed. . . . Even more important may be the role of the third-
> sector institution in creating . . . a sphere of meaningful citizenship.[17]

However the relationship of third-sector institutions to the community
is characterized—as human change agent, involving college, interactive
institution, or any other number of descriptors—the urban college or
university has a mission that is linked to its community. Still, not all
campuses located in urban environments support societal partnerships,
and the degree of involvement varies greatly among them. Some, in fact,
avoid contact as much as possible and work very hard to be clones of more
traditional institutions. Despite vast changes in their student populations
and in the nature and needs of the society they serve, these institutions

cling to the notions of an earlier time and place. The fact that they attempt to impose traditional assumptions on a clientele that does not present traditional characteristics raises questions about their future and their chances for success.

Urban colleges and universities that have embraced the challenges of their role in the new society are often characterized by a fervor and energy not unlike that which the coach observed when he lamented "they are on a mission from God!" While no one would support the notion that urban campuses have somehow been anointed and sent forth to save the society, many do have an urgency about them that is obvious. No doubt this is due, at least in part, to the fact that they are still relatively new. In these institutions change is a daily occurrence, and tradition most often is what one wants it to be. Frank Newman, president of the Education Commission of the States, describes them as institutions that are prime targets for development: "They are sizeable, mainly new, full of older students, yet young by university standards. They are not yet sure of themselves. Their traditions are not so formed that they are barnacled, so that they have a great opportunity to chart a course that serves American society."[18]

GMU's President Johnson notes that such institutions have no history, and therefore they can simply throw themselves into the community. One of the most difficult tasks, he says, is to thwart the natural tendency for academic departments to become rigid along classical lines. "I tell them that I understand why everyone would like to establish precedents," says Johnson. "I know you want to settle down, but it can't happen. It mustn't happen. We're in a trackless area, and we just have to pioneer it."[19] The possibility for real impact and influence in the community and on society is energizing both for faculty and students. In urban institutions it is not unusual to note on program announcements that this or that is the "first annual" event. Because traditions are few and new opportunities with continuing growth and development are many, much of the energy comes from the urgency to do things that need to be done. The constant pace of change and the chance to fulfill potentials are exciting in a profession that is capable of arguing over semicolons for an entire semester.

DIVERSE FACULTY

Urban campuses also are energized by a diverse faculty. Much of the growth of these campuses occurred during a period when an abundance of well-qualified professors were seeking employment. Many urban institutions were able to hire first-rate faculty who in other times might have chosen positions in traditional settings. As a consequence, many institutions were fortunate enough to establish themselves with far better faculties than new institutions might expect to recruit or afford. By the time these campuses had passed through their formative years, either as brand new campuses or older but changing campuses, another stroke of luck assisted them in building and retaining an excellent faculty. A two-person professional family was beginning to be the norm. For husband and wife to find two good professional jobs in the same area—particularly if both were professors—was not an easy task, but it was much easier in a heavily populated area with multiple educational institutions, industrial firms, and corporate headquarters. A megalopolis could provide the two-career family with an attractive opportunity, and urban universities in the same area often worked together to develop dual working arrangements which profited all. Young faculty, able to avoid the cross-country commuting that is common when both husband and wife are professors, had additional time and energy to engage in the academy.

Urban students also bring to these city-based campuses a special energy of their own. For the most part, nobody "sends" New Majority students to college. Whatever their reasons for enrolling—whether for professional growth, college degree, or simply personal fulfillment—they make the choice that education is of value to them. Many pay all of their own educational expenses. Often, they are more mature and are therefore determined to gain from the opportunity of a higher education all that they can. On many urban campuses, large numbers of students are the first in their families to go to college. They enroll believing the university is a special place, and they are willing to invest in it their personal energies and resources. Their dedication to their own success, their faith in education, and their willingness to sacrifice for the goal of a college education is a unique source of vitality for urban campuses.

TRADITIONAL MODELS OF HIGHER EDUCATION

Indicating the qualities of the urban institutions does not imply that traditional institutional models are in any way inadequate for their constituents. Traditional universities have contributed enormously to the growth and strength of American society. Naisbitt and Aburdene point out that despite the fact that the Japanese award the highest proportion of science degrees of any country in the world—68 percent of all degrees awarded as compared with 25 percent in the United States—they recognize that their system of higher education is weak, and thus they have quietly gone about trying to purchase several small U.S. colleges.[20] Asserting that it is not by chance that the United States has 188 Nobel prizewinners while Japan has five, the authors also maintain that the long-range plan is to create environments in which more Japanese students can study in the United States.[21] Despite their contributions to the growth and great strength of American society, traditional universities were based on models that evolved in response to the needs of a much different society. The United States is no longer an agrarian nation. The majority of its people live, work, and study in metropolitan communities. The New Majority needs urban institutions that adequately meet its needs. It is a romantic notion indeed to believe one period of intensive study in late adolescence will be adequate to last a lifetime of a hundred years, especially given the ever-increasing rate of change. Institutions of higher learning near our population centers and designed to deliver instruction in ways the New Majority can access it are as essential to the twenty-first century as were the land-grant colleges and universities in the last century.

As the country continues to change, so must the urban institutions that serve its people. What the asphalt aggies will ultimately become is still somewhat uncertain. Perhaps they will take the tools of the academy—study and inquiry—and organize them in significantly different ways to meet the diverse learning needs that characterize the New Majority. They also may effectively address the longer life-span needs of the learner, the rapid rate at which our store of knowledge increases, the advances of technology, the speed at which equipment becomes obsolete, the demands of an information society, and the economic and global realities of our time. It is still too soon to tell how urban higher education will do. Certainly, new models are emerging and some positive steps toward change already have occurred.

With the majority of the nation's population and virtually all of its minority groups living in urban areas, urban colleges and universities serving cities have experienced firsthand the changes that are sweeping society. Even though they have often not been accorded the status, influence, or the funding that could be anticipated considering the numbers of students they serve, the importance of urban institutions is clear. At this period in history, they are a primary provider of undergraduate education, the principal enroller of minority students, and the support link in research, service, and development for the nation's cities.

In a 1988 address to the University of Illinois trustees, Donald Langenberg called urban colleges and universities the "universities which are where the action will be and which also choose to be a part of it." Said Langenberg:

> For better or worse, the future of our country will largely be deter-mined by the economic and social success or failure of its cities. . . Increasingly, those universities which will occupy center stage are those which are both *in* and *of* our cities. . . . They may be private or public. Among them are public institutions distinguished by their spirit, their size, their relative youth, and their trajectories. These universities are bringing to the cities the populist land-grant spirit which propelled our older state universities to greatness. They have emerged into the academic mainstream relatively recently, many since World War II. Their trajectories will sooner or later carry many of them into the front ranks of American universities. It is upon these urban universities that the future of our cities, and hence our nation, depends.[22]

REFERENCES

1. Donald N. Langenberg, "Overview: Community Interaction," *Metro-politan Universities* 1 (Fall/Winter 1990–91): 9.

2. Anthony M. Orum, "Apprehending the City: The View from Above, Below, and Behind," *Urban Affairs Quarterly* 26 (4): 594 (June 1991).

3. George D. Kuh et al., eds., *Involving Colleges* (San Francisco: Jossey-Bass, 1991), 105.

4. Walter B. Waetjen and John A. Muffo, "The Urban University: Model for Actualization," *The Review of Higher Education* 6 (Spring 1983): 209.

5. Ibid.

6. Charles E. Hathaway, Paige E. Mulhollan, and Karen A. White, "Metropolitan Universities—Models for the Twenty-First Century," *Metropolitan Universities* 1 (Spring 1990): 15.

7. Ibid.

8. Ernest A. Lynton, "From the Editor's Desk," *Metropolitan Universities* 1 (Spring 1990): 3.

9. J. Wade Gilley, *The Interactive University: A Source of American Revi-talization* (Washington, DC: American Association of State Colleges and Universities, 1990), vii.

10. Maurice D. Weidenthal, ed., "Miami-Dade Community College Vital Statistics, Enrollment Fall 1991," *Urban Community Colleges Report* 2 (January 1991): 4.
11. Shirley Strum Kenny, "Metropolitan Universities and the Multicultural Workforce," *Metropolitan Universities* 1 (Fall/Winter 1990–91): 76.
12. Ronald Lemos, "Advancing Urban Higher Education" (presentation on the California State University System at the National Conference on Urban Higher Education, Cleveland State University, 7 October 1991).
13. Ibid.
14. *University of Louisville 1990-91 Annual Report*, 16.
15. Tom Kazas, "GMU's Road Warriors," *Virginia Business* (August 1989): 23.
16. Peter F. Drucker, *The New Realities* (New York: Harper & Row, 1989), 195–206.
17. Ibid., 204–5.
18. Frank Newman, "Anatomy of the Urban University," *Metropolitan Universities* 1 (Fall/Winter 1990–91): 97.
19. Paula Odin, "GMU's Gospel of Interaction," *Virginia Business* (August 1989): 22.
20. John Naisbitt and Patricia Aburdene, *Megatrends 2000: Ten New Directions for the 1990s* (New York: Avon Books, 1990; reprint, New York: William Morrow, 1990), 209 (page citations are to Avon edition).
21. Ibid., 24, 209.
22. Donald N. Langenberg, "A Voice from the Catacombs" (an address to the University of Illinois Board of Trustees, 9 March 1988).

CHAPTER
three
❀ ❀ ❀ ❀ ❀ ❀ ❀ ❀

Urban Students: The New and Continuing Majority

Urban colleges and universities are confronted with challenges that set them apart from their sister institutions located away from the hurly-burly of America's cities. Not the least of these is the challenge of meeting the widely varying needs of enormously diverse student populations. In that regard, however, some prevalent misconceptions exist about the nature of urban campus diversity.

MISCONCEPTIONS ABOUT URBAN STUDENTS

Among these misconceptions is the notion that nearly all urban students are "nontraditional," that is, adults returning to school who work, are enrolled in school part-time, and commute to class in the evening or on weekends. While it is true that a large number of students fit this definition, with percentages varying greatly from campus to campus, it also is true that nationally about one-half of all students at urban colleges and universities fall in the traditional 18- to 22-year-old age-group.[1]

Another misconception requiring clarification is the notion that urban campuses serve only the economically deprived, who simply cannot afford to go away to school; and the academically underprepared, whose high school grade-point averages and Scholastic Aptitude Test scores are not good enough to gain them entry to "really good" institutions to which they would prefer to go. Inherent in this misconception are several inaccuracies.

First of all, although it is true that urban colleges and universities provide a front-line point of access for many students who rely heavily on government loans or must work to help pay for their education, or both, many students enrolled at most urban campuses receive no financial aid.

Indeed, urban students are frequently supported throughout their college years in the same time-honored way as students at nonurban institutions—by their parents.

Secondly, while a substantial number of students are admitted to urban campuses provisionally, either because they are adults returning to school with academic skills dulled by years of nonuse, or because they are traditional-age students who for a variety of reasons are underprepared for college-level work, many students come to urban campuses with exemplary academic backgrounds. An analysis of data collected by at least one group—the Urban Student Affairs Data Exchange Network—suggests that first-time freshmen enrolling at urban campuses enter the university with performance measure scores that are more than minimally respectable. In the fall of 1990, for example, data collected by this 18-member urban campus consortium indicated that nearly 58 percent of entering freshmen who had taken the American College Test (ACT) scored 20 or above out of a possible 35 points on the composite ACT, and slightly more than 19 percent scored 25 or above. Reports on Scholastic Aptitude results were less conclusive since only eight of the 18 institutions reported SAT outcomes as compared with 17 who reported ACT results.[2]

Most urban higher education institutions offer nonneed-based scholarships to students who excel academically. In fact, at my own institution, in the fall of 1990, 53 percent of the grant and scholarship dollars awarded were based on criteria other than need. Since that time, the GAR Foundation has given the University of Akron a $1.25 million grant to be used primarily to create new endowed scholarships.

Many urban scholars participate in foreign-studies programs, earn prestigious awards, and distinguish themselves in graduate studies. A prime example is a Rhodes Scholar finalist who was a former student of mine. She graduated fourth in her high school class of more than 600 and spent her summers as a teenager studying at a private university away from home. Upon graduation she enrolled at her local urban campus, where she earned an endowed fellowship, completed an undergraduate degree program in two years, graduated with high honors, earned a second undergraduate degree with high distinction a year later, and went on to study for a master's degree at a private college in the East. For this student, financial need was not the decision-making factor in choice of university. Neither was her own academic background. Her decision, she says, was based upon her perception that the urban campus located close to home could offer her excellent opportunities for learning and a college education that was first-rate in quality. She also learned that the urban campus structure allowed for flexibility as she pushed ahead to her goals. One of those was to take more than 30 science credit hours in a single semester, an academic milestone she marked with straight A's.

In some respects this student's pathway to achievement is ui que, but the standard of excellence she reflects is characteristic of many students at urban colleges and universities. U.S. Congressman Peter J. Visclosky is a another example of achievement at an urban campus. Visclosky earned his undergraduate degree in accounting at Indiana University's Northwest campus in Gary, went on to earn a law degree at Notre Dame University and an L.L.M. degree in international and comparative law from Georgetown University. In 1990 he was named by *Roll Call*, an influential Capitol Hill tabloid, as one of the 10 smartest members of Congress.[3]

Examples of urban college and university students who have and do excel are common. While statistics are sparse, my experience and the experiences of colleagues at urban institutions across the country substantiate this fact. Hopefully, in the near future, assessment efforts now underway at many campuses will produce new data to support what those of us who serve in urban higher education observe with regularity. Obviously, traditional students, students with exemplary high school scholastic records, and students who have adequate financial support comprise a significant portion of the diverse populations attracted by urban campuses. The proportions of their representation vary from campus to campus and change as rapidly as the city itself changes. As demographic, economic, and cultural shifts occur in the society, they are often reflected first in the cities and almost simultaneously in the educational institutions located in close proximity. As an increasingly larger percentage of the nation's population is concentrated in the relatively small land area we characterize as urban, those institutions of higher education situated in "urbia" are, in a very real sense, microcosms of the cities and suburbs they serve.

WHO ARE THE URBAN STUDENTS?

Unlike the populations of nonurban campuses, which remain predominantly traditional, the populations of urban campuses reflect an increasing number of older students. Many are the first in their families to go to college. Many are displaced workers seeking to upgrade their knowledge and talents in order to maintain a viable place in the intensely competitive and rapidly changing workplace. Most turn to the urban campus intermittently, taking courses when time, money, personal, and family obligations permit. Many are professionals—physicians, attorneys, health care administrators, accountants, engineers, and educators—who return to campus for postgraduate studies that will help them keep abreast in their respective fields (see Figure 3.1).

Another phenomenon of urban colleges and universities is that many enrollees are women—single parents, divorcees with family obligations, young women with career aspirations, older women facing the empty-nest syndrome, married women seeking to prepare themselves to contribute to the family income, or women who now have time to fulfill their educational dreams (see Figure 3.2). Describing the 1990s as the "decade of women in leadership," Naisbitt and Aburdene note that for the last 20 years U.S. women have taken two-thirds of the new jobs created in the information era and are starting new businesses twice as fast as men. They also write that the percentage of women physicians has doubled since 1972 and that women are earning 13 times more engineering degrees than in 1975.[4] In each of those fields they will require additional education to remain current.

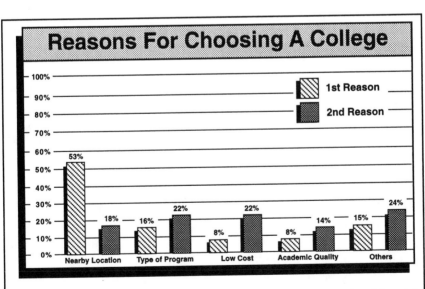

FIGURE 3.1 In a major study by the College Board, more than 70 percent of the adult students surveyed listed convenient location as a primary reason for choosing a college.

Source: Carol B. Aslanian and Henry M. Brickell, eds., *How Americans in Transition Study for College Credit*, The College Board, 1988, 56.

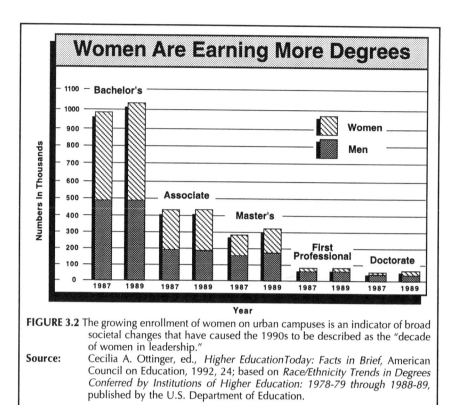

FIGURE 3.2 The growing enrollment of women on urban campuses is an indicator of broad societal changes that have caused the 1990s to be described as the "decade of women in leadership."

Source: Cecilia A. Ottinger, ed., *Higher EducationToday: Facts in Brief*, American Council on Education, 1992, 24; based on *Race/Ethnicity Trends in Degrees Conferred by Institutions of Higher Education: 1978-79 through 1988-89*, published by the U.S. Department of Education.

The growing participation of women in the work force, and in education, is fueled in part by labor force needs. Naisbitt and Aburdene point out that in the next decade 14 or 15 million new jobs will be created, but the labor supply will increase less than 1 percent per year, the slowest growth it has experienced since the 1930s. They also maintain that corporations will be forced to recruit people who did not work during the 1980s and that the largest single potential source of untapped labor supply is the estimated 14 million nonworking women who have been caring for their families at home.[5] This megatrend is reflected in growing female enrollments, with the ratio of females to males running as high as three-to-one on some urban campuses. Women now earn a majority of the B.A. and M.A. degrees awarded and more than a third of the doctorates and first professional degrees.[6]

In returning to school, women often encounter challenges that require a broad range of campus support services, including child care, academic and personal counseling, flexible course schedules, financial assistance, mentoring, and networking opportunities. In fact, for many women, financial aid turns out to be as complex an issue as it is an essential one for success. The case of a divorced mother of six who struggled to feed and clothe her children with food stamps and welfare assistance is illustrative of that complexity. The student, who celebrated her 48th birthday with a college degree and an opportunity to control her own destiny, encountered many difficulties when she enrolled at the urban university near her home. Among the most difficult was a reduction in her food-stamp allowance when she received state and federal student assistance funds. Nevertheless, she says she persevered because "I wanted to do something positive for me and my children. I wanted them to see the value of a college education, and I didn't want to work in a factory."

This New Majority student graduated with a more than respectable grade-point average, she established a special support group for returning students, and was appointed by the governor of her state to serve on the Student Assistance Commission. When it comes to determination, she is not unlike many of her university classmates. Her experience reflects that of several significant enrollment trends at urban campuses across the country. An older student, she is a single parent, a female, a member of a minority group, and a person who has juggled home responsibilities and course assignments with part-time jobs to support her family. While traditional high school graduates represent about half of the enrollment on most urban campuses, this student is representative of the other half, the New Majority students who add to higher education's diversity.

In many ways she also is a mirror image of the campus profile painted by a recent College Board survey, which revealed a continuing increase in the number of older adults on campus, more than half of whom are women, 85 percent who hold jobs, and only about 15 percent who expect to graduate within four years.[7] Based on demographic trends and its own surveys, the College Board predicts that within 10 years older students will constitute an urban campus majority. On some urban campuses older adults already are a majority. In fact, commencement ceremonies at these institutions offer ample evidence that the so-called generation gap is closing, with high school graduates, working adults, and senior citizens shedding their descriptors of identity to take on the new status of college or university student.

Another student, now a nurse, and her son, now a schoolteacher, are classic examples. A widow, she lost her husband to a heart attack. Ten years later she collected her bachelor's degree in nursing on the same stage with her 29-year-old son, who earned his degree in education.

This New Majority student made the bold leap from homemaker to student just six weeks after her husband died. "You just pick yourself up by your bootstraps and go on," she said. "I had five children. What choice did I have?" She started her decade-long educational odyssey with LPN courses at the local technical college, worked part-time at a hospital, and earned an associate degree six years before she completed requirements for her bachelor's degree. During her years on campus this student and her son would meet in the library or the student center to discuss tests, term papers, and course work deadlines. "You're always there for each other," she explained, noting that as university students she and her son shared a common identity and often faced the same pressures.

The trend to older populations on urban campuses is not simply a reflection of a middle-age learning phenomenon. Increasingly, as they retire earlier and live longer, people are turning to their neighborhood colleges and universities for learning opportunities that put leisure time to productive use. Additionally, according to Naisbitt and Aburdene, one of the potential labor sources of the 1990s is the estimated 3.3 million workers who have taken early retirement.[8] Some retirees enroll in non-credit classes, some come to study subjects they always wanted to learn about, some come to upgrade their knowledge for re-entry into the labor force, and some simply enroll to fulfill the lifelong dream of earning a degree. A prime example can be found in John Kirchhoff, who returned to the classroom at age 60 to study nursing.[9] A retired Navy engineer, having spent more than 30 years designing and building ships, Kirchhoff had helped his wife study for the nursing profession 20 years ago. She worked as a licensed practical nurse for 18 years before illness forced her to quit. Kirchhoff cared for her at home until her death, after which their family doctor asked him what he was going to do. When Kirchhoff replied that he was considering becoming a nurse's aide, the doctor challenged him to "go for broke" and become a registered nurse. Now, he has passed the halfway mark toward a new career. "At my age, when most people retire, they want to travel and take it easy," Kirchhoff told *Community College Week* reporter Joye Mercer. "But I've always felt that you've got to keep busy. Otherwise you kind of wither up."

The ability and perseverance of seniors is stereotypically reflected in Eva Corzon Fernando Luma, who at 77 served as the student speaker for Portland Community College's 1991 commencement ceremony.[10] Described as a nontraditional student who epitomizes the heart of the community college mission, Luma, who immigrated to the United States from the Philippines, became a naturalized citizen in 1980. Robert Palmer, PCC dean of student development, said Luma "represents the determination it takes for many of our students to get an education."

About 80 percent of today's urban campus students commute to campus, more than half are enrolled part-time, and although less than a third live with their parents, most of them do not reside in dormitories.[11]

While many college graduates over age 30 cherish fond memories of the sorority rush and freshman beanies, the "rush" for today's urban university students is more likely defined in terms of a mad dash from class to the child-care center to collect their offspring or a rush-hour drive from office to campus for evening classes. The issues that concern these students are practical ones—parking, transportation, traffic, flexible class scheduling, bad weather, the availability and affordability of transportation, utility and housing costs, health insurance, and child care.

Shirley Strum Kenny, president of Queens College, The City University of New York, notes that about 60 percent of her institution's 17,500 students are first-generation college students and at least 80 percent work.[12] The majority, she says, are women, 40 percent are minorities, and 45 percent are immigrants or the offspring of immigrants. They come from 120 different countries and speak 66 different native languages. The largest ethnic groups are Hispanic Americans, African Americans, Chinese Americans, Korean Americans, Italian Americans, and Greek Americans. Kenny says, "Both business and the academy have in recent times had the attitude that we will open our doors to 'them' to become like us. There are two problems with this attitude: first, 'they' want to be themselves, and second, the 'us' of the United States has changed dramatically. The mythical 'typical American student' is not the one etched in our memories by our own college experiences in a different era—'we' and 'they' are the 'us' of tomorrow."[13]

STUDENTS WITH SPECIAL NEEDS

The fact is, shifting demographics are not just bringing more part-timers, women, minorities, middle age, and older students to urban campuses. They also are bringing students with special needs—the high school valedictorian who needs the challenge of honors courses, the underprepared high school graduate who needs developmental courses and tutoring, the white-collar employee whose displacement by corporate downsizing brings a need for counseling as well as preparation for a new career. The varied needs of an increasingly diverse mix of students are having a dramatic impact on campuses across the country, and, at the very least, will require a new mind set in the academy, fresh approaches to teaching, innovative modes of instructional delivery, and a far greater recognition and understanding of diversity than has been the case in the past.

For those special students whose lives are rooted in urban poverty, a supportive campus environment is particularly important if they are to be successful in college. Many of these students have not had the kind of day-to-day experiences that would foster intellectual development. Even those who are not lagging behind scholastically may find that their own culture and language are so far removed from that of the university community that it is difficult for them to communicate in the academic environment. The clash of cultures can be confusing, even painful. The issue of access is critical in the urban setting where the need for a literate and knowledgeable work force is great, unemployment is high, and, for many, the only opportunity for self-improvement and upward mobility rests with higher education. Some students will not be able to do well at the local college campus, and, sadly, the open-door policy of some urban institutions has become nothing more than a revolving door policy. Still, the problem, particularly acute on urban campuses, is this: How do we determine which students will be able to do well and which will not?

In an article for the *Journal of Developmental Education*, Carlette Hardin, director of developmental studies at Austin Peay State University, Clarksville, TN, says:

> I have had advisees whose ACT and SAT scores would indicate that they should have no hope of earning a degree. And, while these students have to struggle to survive in college, they persist to receive a diploma a few years later. I have advised students with solid college-prep backgrounds who dropped out before the first term was over. I have also taught students, arriving with GED diplomas in hand, who not only graduate from college but do so with honors.[14]

Hardin characterizes developmental students in the following six ways: (1) "poor choosers," those who made a decision or decisions which adversely affected their academic future; (2) adult learners who have been away from the academic setting for an extended period; (3) students who had academic or physical weaknesses that were never detected in high school; (4) students who acquired their elementary and secondary education in a foreign country; (5) students with physical or learning disabilities; and (6) students who lack clear-cut academic goals but simply use the educational system for their own purposes. All of these are found on urban campuses, and all, Hardin insists, have the potential to be successful at the college level.

The "poor choosers" include students who drop out of high school for one reason or another—boredom, marriage, the military, pregnancy, crisis in the family, the need to work—then later decide to return to the academic setting. It also includes those who simply fail to take college preparatory courses in high school either because they did not understand what would be required in college or because someone suggested that they were not "college material." In both cases these students come to the campus underprepared, and, given the opportunity to catch up, often do so quickly, going on to complete successfully one or more degree programs. The same is true for adult learners, many of whom simply need refresher courses.

Students whose physical or academic problems go undetected in high school often have greater difficulty when they reenter the academic environment. Some have vision or hearing difficulties that were unnoticed and that caused them to fall behind. Some simply fail to acquire critical socialization skills and thus have difficulty interacting with their professors or classmates. Foreign students, and others for whom English is a second language, may have difficulty communicating and require special assistance in reading, writing, and vocabulary. Physically handicapped students must deal not just with the usual adjustments that accompany entry into college, but also with braille texts, hearing aids, and wheelchairs. Those who are learning-disabled face other challenges. Their problems are often viewed by professors and peers as signs of laziness, lack of ability, or motivation, and their need for support systems is important.

Students with outstanding high school academic records may also enter the university with special needs. Indeed, many students on urban campuses battle great odds just to get to class each day. Ruth G. Shaw, former president of Central Piedmont Community College in Charlotte, NC, tells of attending a campus reception to honor CPCC's first group of 22 Alexander Scholars.[15] After the ceremonies, picture-taking, and handshaking were over, President Shaw stayed to complete some other tasks, leaving the campus about 8 P.M. Driving home she noticed one of the young women who was an Alexander Scholar still waiting at a bus stop. It was growing dark, and Shaw asked if she could give the young woman a lift. "She looked down, uncertain, then gave a sideways glance at me. 'You may not want to take me where I live. I can just take the bus from the square.'" When the young woman provided her street address, CPCC's

President recognized it as an area where crime and violence were common.

Shaw tells how she drove the student home through neighborhoods of urban blight, with rundown housing, weeds, cars cruising and stopping, people on porches, and children playing in the streets at dusk. "This young woman full of promise had come alone on the bus to the reception featuring tiny sandwiches on silver trays, set in our lovely Quad dining room, in the midst of a beautifully manicured campus." Shaw added, "There is a vast distance from her life in the shadow of Charlotte to the classrooms at CPCC to the career toward which she aspires. And determined as she is, the barriers can be formidable."[16] Shaw points out that the barriers that throw students off track can be as simple as registration hassles, problems related to college transfer, or even a rude remark. It is in everyday, ordinary interactions, she notes, that urban campuses are able to nourish the hopes and dreams of many students. Academic advising, assistance with registration, help in filling out financial aid papers, a warm smile from a staff or faculty person, peer tutoring, campus and community mentors, internship opportunities, a place to make friends and hang out with fellow students—all are important to eventual success.

The urban student mix is forever changing the face of campuses across the country, creating a coast-to-coast phenomenon. In Florida, at Miami-Dade Community College, more than 70 percent of the students are of Hispanic background, many of them lacking basic language or economic survival skills.[17] In Los Angeles, City College now enrolls students who speak 62 different languages and whose levels of education and ability represent the entire academic spectrum. People in neighborhoods around the college have come by the thousands in recent years from Latin America and from the Far East. While Miami-Dade is challenged by newcomers from Nicaragua and other Latin American countries, Los Angeles City College is serving the largest Korean population outside the Far East.[18]

LIFELONG LEARNING

Another noticeable characteristic of today's urban colleges and universities, as noted earlier, is the fact that students often are involved with the campus for longer periods of time and take more years to complete degree requirements. Frequently, they alternate periods of school and work, "stopping out," as it is informally called, to fulfill family obligations or pursue other interests or needs. In fact, students who take longer than the traditional four or five years to earn a degree are virtually the norm. Recent studies indicate that only about 15 percent of students at all colleges and universities graduate within four years, and less than half complete an academic program in five years.[19]

John Thames, dean of continuing education at Oglethorpe University in Atlanta, says these are not the "professional" students of yesteryear, the ones who changed majors every two years, collected credit hours for the fun of it, and stayed in school for a decade or more simply because they loved the place.[20] "They're the opposite of the concept of Berkeley—the student who's hanging around because it's a reinforcing environment," Thames told a reporter. "They're like Scarlett O'Hara, down on the dirt saying, 'They're not gong to be kicking me around anymore.' They'll do what it takes."

Typical of this type of student is a student who graduated from high school in 1965, enrolled at her local university campus nearly two decades later, juggled family responsibilities and schoolwork for five years, earned a bachelor's degree in 1991, and is working on a master's degree with an eye toward specializing in neurological critical care. With four children and two grandchildren, this New Majority graduate can best be described as focused, so focused in fact that during her undergraduate years she consistently earned a spot on the Dean's List, all the while teaching in anatomy, physiology, and microbiology labs at the university.

Urban areas with service-oriented job markets tend to "produce" many lifelong learners, people who return to campus time after time to acquire new knowledge that will make it possible for them to advance in the workplace. In cities where manufacturing operations have been closed and new technological and service markets are developing, displaced workers turn to the urban campus for degrees that will lead to new careers. Many of these adult learners are men and women who have already earned degrees in other fields. Some are students who left high school without acquiring the skills needed to succeed in college, while others had solid college preparatory programs in high school but have not used for many years the academic knowledge they acquired. Regardless of their background, most of these students expect that college will move them toward a new and better career in today's competitive marketplace (see Figure 3.3). A. W. Astin, in the annual Cooperative Institutional Research Program report, reveals that nationally college freshmen report that getting a job is a critical issue in their decision to attend college.[21] En route to the goal of a job, students may give little thought to the fact that their lives will likely

Trends In Reasons For Going To College

	1971 Men	1971 Women	1978 Men	1978 Women	1988 Men	1988 Women
To get a better job	77	70	75	76	83	82
To gain a general education and appreciation of ideas	53	67	62	75	54	66
Be able to make more money	57	42	66	55	76	69
Learn about things that interest me	65	74	69	69	78	76
Prepare for graduate or professional school	39	29	44	44	46	53
Nothing better to do	2	2	2	2	3	3

FIGURE 3.3 Regardless of gender, age, or cultural background, most students enroll in college with the expectation that it will help them secure a better job.
Source: Helen S. Astin, "Educating Women: A Promise and a Vision for the Future," *American Journal of Education* 98 (August 1990): 485. First published by the University of Chicago, 1990.

be enriched, even dramatically changed, as a result of the college experience.

Some urban students are like a former student of mine, the son of an Alabama coal miner who became a steel worker and never dreamed of going to college. He grew up in a thriving city where steel was "king" and young people went straight from high school to work in the mills. Following in his father's footsteps he took a job with U.S. Steel at age 17. In the 1960s, the company he worked for was the number-one steel producer worldwide. He thought he was on top of the world. Then came foreign competition, and his company lost its competitive edge. When U.S. Steel's profits took a nose dive, his fortunes headed the same way. Plant officials and outplacement specialists advised steel industry employees that they must retrain, but he and his coworkers didn't want to believe it. "I thought those were some cold people," he recalls. "We wanted to feel sorry for ourselves because the Japanese took away our jobs."

Finding himself too young to be idle but without marketable skills, this New Majority student enrolled in classes at his local university campus, took a part-time job, and decided to pursue a degree in criminal justice. Once on campus, however, he found himself in developmental courses designed to bring his reading, writing, and math skills to acceptable levels. Today, having earned a bachelor's degree and completed course work at the state law enforcement academy, he is a police officer who has found a new niche in life and a new perspective as well. He says having an urban campus close by helped him build a new life. "I am a different person now," he says.

DIVERSITY

Much of what we know about urban campuses and their students is anecdotal, but research is beginning to lay the groundwork for a larger and important body of knowledge. One study, headed by Mary F. Kinnick and Mary F. Ricks at Portland State, is based on two surveys of 32 urban public universities, the first of which was conducted in 1978 and the second in 1987.[22] Using Maurice Berube's theory that urban state universities, like community colleges, are a new kind of institution in American higher education, Kinnick and Ricks set out to determine if there were demonstrable characteristics uniquely common to these institutions. In analyzing trends over the 10-year period, the two researchers verified that the Urban 32 serve a significantly higher proportion of part-time students than all four-year institutions as a group and that the growth rate for part-time students at these institutions was twice as high as that at all four-year public institutions. Moreover, Kinnick and Ricks also found that the Urban 32 experienced a greater growth rate in full-time enrollments.

In 1990 Kinnick and Ricks reported that in terms of institutional development, with respect to access and graduate education, the Urban 32 emerged as distinctly distinguishable from the larger group of American colleges and universities. They have a higher rate of enrollment growth. Most are located in growing metropolitan areas. They are disproportionately serving more part-time students, and their part-time enrollment growth exceeds national averages.[23] Contrary to reports from some campuses, Kinnick and Ricks did not discover proportionate increases in minority student enrollment among the Urban 32. "This surprised and concerned us, given their location and fee levels, commitment to part-time students, and accessibility of evening programs," the researchers wrote, noting they plan to do further study to learn about institutions that appear to have been more successful in attracting minorities.[24]

One campus reporting increased minority participation, however, is California State University—Los Angeles. In fact, Desdemona Cardoza, assistant vice president for information resources management, believes that by the year 2020 most urban colleges and universities in the nation will resemble her own, which, in addition to growing minority representation, has a student body made up of lifelong learners, part-time students, older students, and a greater number of women.[25] Described as the most culturally diverse comprehensive university campus in the state, California State University—Los Angeles, like many other urban campuses, draws from a population that reflects growing numbers of Hispanics, Asians, and African Americans.

By the year 2020, the prediction is that Hispanics will represent approximately 37.7 percent of California's population, Asians 14.2 percent, African Americans 7.5 percent, and whites 40.6 percent. In the first decade of the new century the majority of Californians will be people of color.[26] Cardoza, at a 1991 conference on urban higher education, reported that her campus began experiencing these demographic shifts more than a decade ago and now faces major challenges in fulfilling its mission of providing access and accommodating the diverse needs and learning styles of its students. The challenges, she noted, are overrepresentation of high-risk, underprepared students, inequities in state funding, and faculty who are not prepared to deal with the needs of underprepared students.

Cardoza pointed out that the overwhelming majority of faculty at colleges and universities across the country do not share the same background as the typical student on her campus or, for that matter, those on most urban campuses. "The difference between those who teach and those who are being taught is more than just in terms of race and ethnicity," she said. "It also has to do with income level, family, culture, language background, and cognitive style." Cardoza expressed a belief that most faculty are keenly interested in learning new approaches that will enhance their effectiveness in teaching today's diverse mix of students but noted that this need calls for development programs that are both costly and above and beyond the regular level of faculty development.

Along these lines, a 1990 *Chronicle of Higher Education* article by Beverly Watkins focused on the ways in which the influx of older students in the classroom has caused faculty members to take a closer look at their teaching styles.[27] Chet Meyers, a humanities professor at Metropolitan State University who has many 30- to 40-year-old students in his courses, said the new classroom mix requires that education become "an active enterprise." "Adults don't play the passive-recipient game very well," said Meyers. "I couldn't lecture to my classes. The younger students might sit still for a lecture, but the older students, who have been out of school, would not sit and listen to me pontificate. They would grind their teeth." Watkins also noted that some faculty members are using shorter talks followed by discussions in which students ask and answer questions, while other professors are experimenting with collaborative learning activities, such as organizing panel presentations or dividing their students into small groups.

As evening and weekend classes become increasingly important to urban students, extended campus office hours are more the norm, and even the traditional 14- to 15-week semester calendar is being studied by some to see if part-time learners who attend classes year-round might be better accommodated in some other format or time frame. We know, for example, that adults with multiple responsibilities as spouse, parent, employee, and student may need to attend class one evening a week for three hours rather than three evenings a week for one hour.

CHALLENGES FOR THE URBAN CAMPUS

Urban institutions have a different set of challenges as a result of their location, not the least of which is the difficulty of reaching students outside the classroom as well as those who fail to enroll during a particular semester. Commuting students who come and go at varying hours during weekdays, nights, and on weekends are less likely to interact with the institution in ways that promote the kind of bonding that helps move them toward success. Student activities programming must be varied enough to appeal to the traditional 18- to 22-year-old whose interests include participation in clubs and athletics, dating, and socializing as well as older students whose interests may run the gamut from old movies to programs on parenting or caring for elderly parents.

Fordham University's Lincoln Center campus in Manhattan, where the undergraduate population is approximately 65 percent New Majority, employs a number of approaches to assist students, including evening seminars for adults and part-timers, the addition of upper-class peer leaders, the early introduction of student networking opportunities, workshops on "Choosing a Major," two-hour student activities periods during which no classes are scheduled, expanded hours in the career planning and placement office, and evening hours during which students are invited to meet in informal settings with faculty.[28] The campus also places emphasis on orientation sessions that incorporate a comprehensive career information component and are offered at times that meet the demands of the student population.

Lauren Mounty points out that orientation at the Lincoln Center campus is viewed not only as a function of the student affairs division, but as a university-wide effort designed to aid students academically, socially, and developmentally. In expanding office hours for career planning and placement and in rearranging faculty office hours in the evening, the campus experienced greater success in serving students. "Without expanded hours," Mounty reports, "students who were reached during orientation and student activities periods would find the door locked when they wanted a one-on-one appointment. The services that we strive so hard to provide would be unavailable if the students could not follow through with this process."[29]

Reaching out to increasingly diverse constituencies also makes distance learning important for urban institutions. Computer technology linking students to campus, classes offered via cable television, workplace education with campus and employer computers providing the connection are all technological tools that provide alternative methods for reaching out. One learning-delivery mechanism, Mind Extension University, is a cable network devoted exclusively to education, and it is growing in polularity.[30] Established in 1987, this program already reaches more than a million households, putting a four-year degree within reach of many full-time workers and single parents who cannot easily leave home.

Older students are not the only ones being served by technology, however. In 1991 Jim C. Johnsen, a political science professor at Oklahoma City Community College, introduced videodisks in a course called American Federal Government.[31] "One of the biggest battles I fight is to maintain students' interest," Johnsen said. To capture the interests of a classroom of traditional-age students who cut their teeth on television and the VCR, the Oklahoma City professor uses a videodisk player hooked up to a TV monitor. Since his initial interview with the *Chronicle of Higher Education* in 1991, Johnsen says the potential of video to kindle students' interest in learning has become a source of great excitement at OCCC, where about 20 percent of the faculty are now experimenting with video. "It allows me to bring into the classroom people and events I have only previously been able to talk about," says Johnsen, who adds that if technology is effective in delivering the message and students pay attention to it then, "For Pete's sake, let's use it."

In Maine and Northern Virginia, the community college systems have received funding from the Annenberg/CPB Project to develop complete associate degree programs using distance learning technology, and a growing number of telecourses are being produced by college and university consortia throughout the United States.[32] *Chronicle of Higher Education* reporter Beverly Watkins says students who work and cannot make it to campus during the day are able to use a computer and a modem to pursue a master's degree in business and administration at the University of Phoenix.[33] This urban campus uses a "host" computer called the Apollo Learning Exchange and divides students into groups of 15 who work with an instructor, read lectures, and take their tests at a terminal. Beyond the links for working students, however, computer simulation games, tutorials, and drill and practice exercises are especially useful for others, particularly those who come to the university underprepared. Working alone at a terminal permits them the freedom of making mistakes without the embarrassment of doing so in front of their peers.

In addition to the need for technological linkages, flexible class scheduling, alternatives in instructional delivery, developmental courses, convenient child-care facilities, and faculty who are prepared to challenge and communicate in new ways, commuter students also need to feel they "belong." Increasingly, urban campuses are looking at activities, programming, and facilities that will foster in students a sense of being connected to the campus. Discussions on improving campus climate are held at conferences, and some institutions have established committees or programs to deal with this issue. Lockers, lounge areas, a central message center, food courts, places for students to meet each other, club rooms, recreational facilities, and cooperative learning centers are all important in encouraging students to put down "roots." One urban campus added football a few years ago and now draws more than 20,000 supporters a game whether there is a winning team or not. Many of the support services that foster extracurricular learning on traditional campuses are just as necessary for New Majority students.

Equally important are questions related to financial aid. As Tom Melecki, a research analyst with the Texas Guaranteed Student Loan Corporation in 1984, noted in a journal article: "To achieve true equity in the administration of student financial aid programs, it is not enough to treat all applicants in an equal manner. Students are different, and to achieve the same results, different levels and types of support are required."[34]

Melecki pointed out that the Carnegie Council has suggested a unique approach to the treatment of maintenance costs for dependents of adult learners. Instead of including dependents' costs in budgets, the Council has proposed adult budgets similar to those of traditional students. Dependents' expenses would be allowances in family contribution formulas, similar to those currently accorded to families of dependent students.

Many questions are raised by the current system of financial aid. For example, in a competitive market that requires maximum productivity, it seems to make little sense that a single mother, struggling to feed her family and improve her circumstances, should have food stamp assistance reduced when she receives a Pell Grant to attend her local university campus. Obviously, current financial aid regulations limit access to higher education, particularly at urban institutions, which are the primary point of entry to the economic mainstream for many nontraditional learners. "There are a number of ways people think the system is disadvantageous to older students," says Arthur Hauptman, a consultant to the American Council on Education.[35] Hauptman, who was quoted in an article by *Washington Post* reporter Debbie Goldberg, pointed out that older students have often left a job to return to school. They have fixed living costs and often have families to support, said Hauptman, adding, "There's a feeling that the traditional needs analysis system doesn't recognize the needs of the family while a husband or wife is going to school."

Goldberg went on to say adult students who leave their jobs to enroll at a local college or university, as well as those whose economic status may have changed through divorce, are penalized by the prior-year income rule that is used to determine eligibility for aid. Education consultant Lawrence Gold, whose book, *Campus Roadblocks*, outlines the obstacles that New Majority students face in going to college, characterizes the prior-year income concept as "inherently flawed," and says that because of state regulations and individual caseworker discretion, few unemployed people are able to go to college while collecting benefits.[36] Loans can be a problem, too. Although the most common form of assistance for New Majority students, and often their only option, loans may simply add to the mounting financial burden and delay, or even halt, escape from a cycle of poverty.

SERVING THE NEW MAJORITY

Clearly, urban institutions must carefully research the needs of their students, whether they be academic, personal, or financial. The kinds of knowledge needed involve student costs, resources, kinds of counseling needed, academic programs being sought, times and places that make sense for the delivery of courses, types of financial aid they are receiving, and kinds of aid they are denied. Students also need to be asked about the number of hours spent on campus, whether they have children, whether they need and want campus child care, the kinds of student activities programming they would like to see on campus, how difficult it is for them to register, whether they are able to enroll in classes at times that are convenient to them, and what institutional impediments delay or prevent their success in higher education.

Perhaps the most important question urban college and university administrators might ask is "What benefits do students expect to derive from college or university study?" Clearly, the overwhelming majority of them attend college to prepare for or advance in a career. Indeed, study after study has shown that the ultimate goal of college students is to become gainfully employed. Says Queens College president Kenny: "Faculty of an older generation still talk about education for its own sake, still make the old pronouncements about how liberal arts make one a better and more humane person. But plainly and simply, our students need jobs. They have to help their families; they have to work before or after classes; and few have the leisure to cast aside the economic realities of life to enjoy the pleasures of the mind, unhampered by practical thoughts."[37]

Kenny adds, however, that in preparing students for landing that first job, urban institutions also have an obligation to prepare them for keeping it by providing a strong undergraduate education with a firm foundation in the liberal arts. To that end, Queens College has developed a combination business and liberal arts degree program that couples a major in whatever liberal arts field the student chooses with a minor in business-related subjects. The program, developed with input from an advisory board made up of corporate representatives, also includes an internship component to give students practical experience while they are working toward a degree.

Ultimately, the success of urban colleges and universities is, of course, measured by the improved circumstances and the productive lives of their students. Whether those students come to campus at age 18 or 80, well prepared or ill prepared, with or without families to support, with great or minimal financial resources, the bottom line is what happens to them once they complete their studies and leave the campus. August Souza Kappner, former president of the Borough of Manhattan Community College, the largest of seven colleges in the City University of New York, tells the story of walking along a Manhattan street one day when a Federal Express truck driver recognized her.[38] The woman driving the truck pulled over, jumped out, and said, "President Kappner, I just wanted you to know that I graduated from BMCC. I'm driving this truck part-time and I'm a pre-med student." Kappner says it reminded her of what she loves most about her job, knowing that students' lives are being forever changed by their education at BMCC.

As urban institutions work to meet the needs of diverse and changing student populations, it is important that they examine those needs in positive and creative ways. "Too many institutions face the future looking at students of diverse background in terms of their deficits rather than their assets," says Herman Blake, vice chancellor for Student Affairs, Indiana University—Purdue University at Indianapolis.[39] "Often we look at students and use negative terminology such as culturally deprived, or high need, or low preparation. It's very difficult and sometimes very insulting for students to be defined in terms of what they don't have." Blake recalls how one determined student told him of studying at night while pedaling her exercise bicycle. She knew it was time to go to bed, she said, when she fell asleep. Suggesting that colleges and universities build an asset model of urban, commuting students, Blake says, "If we begin to look at our students in terms of the assets or the positive strengths and characteristics they bring to us, we see very often an extraordinary group of people. Our thinking often has prevented us from taking advantage of those extraordinary characteristics."[40]

Ronald Lemos, dean of Business and Economics at California State University—Los Angeles, in a 1991 presentation on urban campuses, said CSU is examining the mission of its urban campuses in terms of the educational pipeline concept, realizing there are "leakages" at every point.[41] "We lose prospective college students at all points throughout the educational pipeline," Lemos explained, "whether it's inadequate training or preparation for training at K-6 in math and science or inadequate preparation in the middle or high school." Noting that campuses formerly focused on recruiting incoming freshmen at the junior or senior year of high school, Lemos recalled how they discovered that they needed to start earlier and dropped back to the tenth grade, but found that that was too late, too. "We went into the middle school," he says, "and that was too late in terms of developing a future cadre of students. Now we're convinced that we have to start at K-6, and even earlier in terms of making sure that students get adequately prepared for a college education."

To do this CSU is focusing on its primary role as the preparer of approximately 70 percent of the newly credentialed teachers prepared in California. "All of our children are taught by teachers, so this is a very important mission," Lemos says, adding that the mission is complicated by the fact that California teachers are frequently assigned to classrooms where several different primary languages are spoken by the students, and where the first-year teacher attrition rate for some areas is as high as 40 percent.[42]

The success of teacher education reform efforts, coupled with solid linkages between urban colleges and the public schools, is increasingly critical to the life and vigor of the nation's cities. It is important to realize, too, that the trends now having a dramatic impact on urban education at all levels will not suddenly reach a cutoff point next year or in the year 2000, but will continue to be felt well into the next century. Among these is the decline in U.S. population growth, which, although it has reached an historical low, is not being reflected among minority groups, who are experiencing a growth rate two to 14 times greater than the nonminority population.[43] Over the next 20 years, the 18- to 24-year-old age-group from which colleges and universities have traditionally drawn students is expected to decrease by more than five million. Among Hispanics and African Americans, however, that same age-group is expected to increase from 5.2 million to 6.6 million. Given a declining overall pool of traditional college-age youth, if urban colleges and universities are to maintain enrollments and adequately serve the communities in which they are located, they will be forced not only to actively recruit minority students and older adults but also to restructure academic programming and student services to accommodate the needs of all students.

In the past, colleges and universities—urban and nonurban alike—generally absorbed nontraditional students with strategies aimed at encouraging them to adapt to the institution's traditional language and culture.

As Indiana University professor Eileen Bender puts it: "Our task was to make their difference whether in age, race, gender, or ethnic background invisible." Where previously the university felt its mission was to bring nontraditional students into the mainstream, Bender points out, the institution is now dealing with a new reality. "The news . . . is that this diverse student body is the mainstream."[44]

In *The New Realities* Drucker maintains that the educational system needed for today's knowledge society must be an open one that does not make into an impenetrable barrier the line between the highly schooled and the "other half." Asserting that education fuels the economy and shapes the society through its "product," the educated person, Drucker says that in the knowledge society there is no such thing as a "finished education." Lifelong learning is a requirement, and people with advanced schooling must return for education again and again.[45]

As microcosms of the society and as institutions best located to serve society's educational needs, urban colleges and universities bear a unique responsibility in preparing citizens for life in this very different world.

REFERENCES

1. Association for the Study of Higher Education, *Students in Urban Settings*, Report 6 (Washington, DC, 1985), 14.

2. *Student Affairs Data Exchange Urban Public Universities, 1990–92 Reports* (project of the Urban Student Affairs Data Exchange Network; Sandy MacLean, University of Missouri—St. Louis, chairman; Data Services by John Minter Associates, Inc., Boulder, CO), 114–18. This is a confidential report for use by members of the Data Exchange Network.

3. Craig Wisneker, *Roll Call* (Washington, DC), 5 March 1990, 22.

4. John Naisbitt and Patricia Aburdene, *Megatrends 2000: Ten New Directions for the 1990s* (New York: Avon Books, 1990; reprint, New York: William Morrow, 1990), 228–56 (page citations are to Avon edition).

5. Ibid., 244.

6. Gary Orfield, "Public Policy and College Opportunity," *American Journal of Education* (August 1990): 320. First published by the University of Chicago, 1990.

7. Drew Jubera (Cox News Service), "College Students Staying Longer," *The Fort Wayne (Ind.) Journal-Gazette*, 16 July 1991, D6.

8. Naisbitt and Aburdene, *Megatrends 2000*, 244.

9. Joye Mercer, "Grandfather of Three Returns to College, Opts for Nursing Career," *Community College Week* [Portland (Oregon) Community College], 20 January 1992, 6.

10. Linda A. Powell, "Commencement Exercises Mirror Campus Clientele," *Community College Week* [Portland (Oregon) Community College], 27 May 1991, 7.

11. Barbara Jacoby, "Adapting the Institution to Meet the Needs of Commuter Students," *Metropolitan Universities* 1 (Fall/Winter 1990–91): 61.

12. Shirley Strum Kenny, "Metropolitan Universities and the Multicultural Workforce," *Metropolitan Universities* 1 (Fall/Winter 1990–91): 75.

13. Ibid., 83.

14. Carlette Hardin, "Accessible Higher Education: Who Belongs?" *Journal of Developmental Education* 12 (September 1988): 2–4, 6.

15. Ruth G. Shaw, "Giving Students a Lift in More Ways Than One," *Urban Community Colleges Report* 2 (November 1991): 3.
16. Ibid.
17. Maurice D. Weidenthal, "Who Cares about the Inner City? The Community College Response to Urban America," (Washington, DC: Association of Community and Junior Colleges, 1989), 5, 12.
18. Ibid.
19. Jubera, "College Students Staying Longer," D6.
20. Ibid.
21. Lauren H. Mounty, "Involving Nontraditional Community Students in the Career Planning Process at an Urban Institution," *Journal for Higher Education Management* 6 (Winter/Spring, 1991): 43–48.
22. Mary K. Kinnick and Mary F. Ricks, "The Urban Public University in the United States: An Analysis of Change, 1977–1987," *Research in Higher Education* 31 (1): 15–38 (1990).
23. Ibid.
24. Ibid., 36.
25. Desdemona Cardoza, "Advancing Urban Higher Education" (presentation on the California State University System at a National Conference on Urban Higher Education, Cleveland State University, 7 October 1991).
26. Ibid.
27. Beverly T. Watkins, "Growing Number of Older Students Stir Professors to Alter Teaching Styles," *Chronicle of Higher Education* 1 August 1990, A1–A12.
28. Mounty, "Involving Nontraditional Community Students in the Career Planning Process at an Urban Institution," 45.
29. Ibid.
30. Beverly T. Watkins, "Universities Join Effort to Offer Bachelor's Degrees in Management, Entirely through Cable Television," *Chronicle of Higher Education*, 25 September 1991, A-18.
31. Beverly T. Watkins, "Technology Update," *Chronicle of Higher Education*, 25 September 1991, A-21.
32. "Community Colleges Combine Technologies to Advance Distance Learning," compiled from reports by Carol Cross and James Michael Brodie, *Community College Week* [Portland (Oregon) Community College], 22 July 1991, 7.
33. Watkins, "Technology Update," A-30.
34. Tom Melecki, "Adult Learners in Postsecondary Education: Issues for the Student Financial Aid Administrator," *The Journal of Student Financial Aid* 14 (Spring 1984): 12.
35. Debbie Goldberg, "Hitting the Books Late: How Older Students Pay the Bills," *Washington Post*, Education Review Section, 18 Novem-

    ber 1990, 12–13.
36. Ibid.
37. Kenny, "Metropolitan Universities and the Multicultural Workforce,"
    77.
38. Joye Mercer, "Spotlight on Community College Leaders: Augusta
    Kappner Inspired by 'Incredible Function' of CCs," *Community
    College Week* [Portland (Oregon) Community College], 2 Septem-
    ber 1991, 17.
39. Herman Blake, "Urban Higher Education: Prescriptions for the Fu-
    ture" (keynote address at a National Conference on Urban Higher
    Education, Cleveland State University, 7 October 1991).
40. Ibid.
41. Ronald Lemos, "Advancing Urban Higher Education" (presentation
    on the California State University System at a National Confer-
    ence on Urban Higher Education, Cleveland State University, 7
    October 1991).
42. Ibid.
43. Leobardo F. Estrada, "Anticipating the Demographic Future," *Change*
    (May/June 1988): 14, 16–19.
44. Eileen T. Bender, "Indiana University: Adjusting the Educational
    'Fit'," *Policy Perspectives*, Indiana University, Bloomington, IN (No-
    vember 1991).
45. Peter F. Drucker, *The New Realities* (New York: Harper & Row,
    1989), 233–52.

CHAPTER
four

Urban Faculty:
The Asphalt Intelligentsia

The postwar industrial society has come to an end, and the new world we live in is centered on information. It is no secret that the incredible explosion in knowledge during the last quarter of this century is owed, in no small way, to the scientific and technological research efforts of the faculties at U.S. colleges and universities. The breakthroughs fueled by this research have occurred in such number and so rapidly that the rush of society toward innovation is nothing less than mind-boggling. As former Harvard University president Derek Bok has pointed out, it took the Harvard library 275 years to accumulate its first million books, but the latest million was acquired in five short years.

The copper wire that was the standby of telecommunications for years could carry 48 conversations at once; today a single fiber-optic cable can carry more than eight thousand conversations, and by the year 2000 it will be able to transmit 10 million.[1] The development of computer information systems and laser technology, coupled with great strides in life-enhancing health care resulting from discoveries in genetics and biotechnology can be largely credited to faculty research. In the years following World War II, higher education in the United States established itself as the world producer of new knowledge. Indeed, it was the thirst for knowledge—this drive toward discovery—along with the availability of education for most of the nation's citizens that earned American higher education an enviable reputation throughout the world.

FOCUS ON LEARNING

While teaching and research, in their purest sense, must continue to play the significant role in the life of U.S. colleges and universities, other intellectual demands also are emerging in higher education. The advent of knowledge is occurring so rapidly that it has overtaken us; in the race to acquire information none of us can keep pace. As Lindsay Desrochers and Don Detmer have pointed out in an eloquent essay on the "unisearchity," "the knowledge revolution has outstripped the ability of any single individual or institution to 'know it all.'"[2] The new priority in higher education is the transfer of knowledge, and with that priority comes another, the overriding need to teach people how to learn so that they can continually update the knowledge they have acquired.

The emphasis now must be on learning. Those who teach will need to understand the many ways that people learn. Their role will be to facilitate learning—to lead and to encourage rather than primarily to convey the subject matter itself. Just as the printed book triggered a revolution in learning in the fifteenth century, so too is the new technology of this age creating a revolution. Drucker describes it this way:

> In developed countries most people live in metropolitan areas. Thus the learner is no longer confined to the one school with its one learning and teaching pedagogy for everybody, which was all the small village could support. The learner can choose between schools within easy reach, on foot, by bicycle, or by bus. . . . It will become the responsibility of tomorrow's teacher to identify the way learners learn and to direct them to whichever of the available schools best fits their individual learning profiles.[3]

Located as they are, in close proximity to 80 percent of the population, urban colleges and universities are evolving as institutions that have the opportunity to accommodate a broad range of learning styles. Indeed, by the very nature of their diversity, with student populations that constantly shift, urban campuses have already amassed considerable experience in learning styles. Further, urban campuses are uniquely prepared to address the changing priorities of the knowledge society. Having evolved from a multitude of sources—research universities located in or near cities, branch campuses of state universities, and colleges founded and supported by municipalities, to name a few—urban institutions, by nature of their location and mission, have attracted and nurtured faculty who live in and experience the city's diversity. Urban faculty understand the university's multiple constituents. They know the needs, challenges, and opportunities of the city, and they frequently engage in research and service activities that will benefit it. The concept of the ivory tower that often has separated faculty at nonurban institutions from direct involvement with the major issues and problems of society is not so prevalent on urban campuses, where many faculty literally have the opportunity to "do it all"—teach, conduct research in their fields, counsel, tutor, and mentor; serve on the police commission, the housing authority, the hospital and school board; consult with financial institutions; be a member of the symphony or the opera; exhibit paintings and sculptures, and much more. That is not to say that all of their research and activity is limited by the needs of the city or even always associated with urban concerns. Not all fields are urban. It would be nonsense to claim such a limitation. However, for those fields that are related to or are richly nourished by cities—the arts, the social sciences, the professions—they provide a wellspring of valuable data and opportunity.

Based on a study of 14 institutions, both urban and nonurban, Indiana University's George Kuh and his fellow authors of *Involving Colleges* explore five sets of factors and conditions that result in multiple opportunities for students to experience positive and educationally beneficial interaction with faculty, campus life, and—most particularly in urban institutions—the community.[4] One major premise of Kuh is that involvement is the key to learning and that campuses where students are actively involved with faculty, both in and out of the classroom, are those in which students are likely to experience greater success in learning as well as personal development.

MISCONCEPTIONS ABOUT URBAN FACULTY

Patricia R. Plante, former president of the University of Southern Maine, has written about three notions concerning urban faculty that could be classified as myths.[5] First is the idea that serious scholarship is the exclusive province of research university faculty; second, that the nature of scholarship pursued by faculty in urban colleges and universities is somehow less worthy than that pursued by faculty in research universities; and third, that urban faculty should structure and teach courses that are of immediate economic usefulness to their students, even to the neglect of those that have lasting and universal significance. All three ideas are inaccurate, Plante points out, and are only traps "designed specifically to ensnare academic climbers and/or those prone to seek in apathy refuge from hierarchical systems."

In an article the same author paints a picture of faculty needed in the new knowledge-based society:

> Central . . . to the challenges of a metropolitan university is the
> wisdom of attracting and selecting faculty who, throughout their
> professional careers, can give a novel, a theory, a rendition, a perfor-
> mance, a solution "more life than life has"—to use Toni Morrison's
> fine phrase. . . . A monkish Mr. Chipps, however nostalgically endear-
> ing, will not do. The times and the broad mission of a metropolitan
> university, with its rainbow curricula, heterogenous population, and
> demanding complex communities, call for faculty who are both worldly
> and idealistic, who are both sophisticated and caring, who are both
> aware of their own worth and the worth of their students.[6]

Professors who fit this description can be found in abundance, both at
urban and nonurban campuses, but in the metropolitan milieu, abstrac-
tion may be less likely to thrive in the face of challenge from adult
learners. Classroom diversity may more likely foster meaningful engagement between those who teach and those who learn. As Plante puts it,
"Metropolitan university faculty must find ways to empower their students
to discover satisfying patterns not only at the end of syllogisms, but also at
the end of rainbows."[7]

A classic example of the "asphalt intelligentsia" that characterizes
urban faculty is found in Chicago artist David Klamen, who, despite the
fact that his international reputation as a painter moves him in a jet-set
mode from continent to continent, still understands that being worldly
does not require the sacrifice of idealism, and that sophistication is not
incompatible with caring for those who also want to find artistic expres-
sion. Klamen, who thrives in the hustle and bustle of the city, systemati-
cally leaves the solitude of his studio loft and drives through miles of
landscape dotted with housing projects, vacant lots, affluent neighborhoods, giant shopping malls, and smoke-belching factories to teach on an
urban university campus. In the metropolitan landscape he says he finds
excitement; in its students he finds a richness of culture and inquisitive
spirit.

In the classroom Klamen encourages his students toward the same kind
of creativity and self-exploration that are the bedrock of his own artistic
and intellectual pursuits. He teaches that art has a great deal to do with
people's experience and natural insights, their ambitions, ability to be
perceptive and sensitive, understanding of their culture, and their history.
It is, in fact, the resources of the city—museums, galleries, governmental
institutions, health-care facilities, corporate structures, business connections, and industrial complexes—that often draw faculty to urban campuses. As Klamen puts it, "There is no way I could teach in a different

environment. Here I have access to the richness of diverse cultures and to the artistic and business life of the city. I love teaching. It is an important part of making my work."[8]

However the cities' colleges and universities are defined, their faculties have many things in common. Not the least of these is an awareness of the multiple concerns of the communities that exist in close proximity—the environment, housing, health care, government, needs of the elderly, changes in the family, equity in the system of criminal justice, corporate restructuring, unemployment, and so forth. The late Rev. Timothy Healy, former president of Georgetown University, reminded us that the urban university, being *of* and *in* the city faces a reality that votes as heavily as do senior faculty. In a commencement address at Virginia Commonwealth University (see the epilogue), he put it this way:

> The rhythms of trade and commerce impose themselves even on the life of the university, and once out of class its students face the hard and demanding deadlines of jobs. . . . [T]he city never lets its universities escape its most priceless lesson, the correctives of facts and pain. . . . A walk around any city can douse the ebullience of youth and curb the arrogance of learning.[9]

Unfortunately, a caste system continues to exist in higher education that ascribes the most important scholarly status to those educators who do only basic research. For many university faculty this type of research has been the only kind that *really* mattered. In reality, all good research is valuable. Today the intervening time between the discovery of knowledge and its application is so short that the lines between pure and applied research are becoming increasingly blurred, so much so, in fact, that the debate over their relative value is generally pointless. In the cities' evolving colleges and universities, even faculty research of a traditional nature may be transferred quickly to the community, and the question of which is more important—the acquisition or the advancement of knowledge—may be impossible to answer. The complexity and importance of the subject studied and the quality of the research are the final determinants in any case.

Scholarly research takes all kinds of stimulating and useful directions on any campus. The notion that the size or location of the university somehow defines the importance of faculty inquiry is incorrect. In an increasing number of fields, significant scholarly activity is not place-bound. While the historical model involved a group (often called a critical mass) of scholars researching one field, in one place, and with a group of doctoral students for support, it is not the only productive model. Today, technology allows interaction between scholars in such rapid and detailed ways that quite often physical proximity is irrelevant. A "group" may be four scholars, each located in a different state. Earlier I coauthored another book using telephone, fax, computer, and cassette-tape linkages to my colleague in another city. Obviously, some instrumentation and specialized laboratories do continue to be place-bound, but computer simulation models now make it possible for even highly specialized scientific experimentation to be conducted in collaborative ways that are not place-bound. Indeed, breakthroughs in technology and its availability for the transfer and treatment of data have enormously enhanced the scope of scholarship for campuses with or without doctoral students.

While some campuses do not define their faculty as both scholars and teachers, most of them do. Although many community colleges do not provide the same level of faculty research support as do their urban university counterparts, it would be incorrect to assume that faculty of those institutions do not engage in research activity. Scholarly inquiry is no more mission-bound than it is place-bound.

Perhaps the greatest myth involving faculty scholarship promulgates the notion that those located in the "urban laboratory" focus only on problems and needs of the city, and that their research in that regard has produced little that is of positive benefit to cities. Despite the criticisms of Peter Szanton, Washington, DC, policy consultant and former Rand Institute president, and the fact that some formal city-university partnerships have failed, the positive outcomes of less formal relationships between urban faculty and America's cities have received little attention and are woefully underdocumented.[10] While the Ford Foundation's lead program officer, William Pendleton, may have spoken accurately when he reviewed the Foundation's $36 million urban extension program of the 1960s and concluded that "universities and city governments do not work easily together," abundant evidence across the country supports the idea that urban faculty and urban residents, including government leaders, are working together with ease and great success.[11]

While such faculty-city interaction begs for further exploration and documentation, one case in point comes readily to mind. Mark A. Glaser, former assistant professor at Wichita State University's Hugo Wall Center for Urban Studies, began working closely with local government and community groups several years ago, studying governmental structure and policy as well as major issues facing the city. The relationship as academician and practitioner led him eventually to a position as special assistant to the city manager. He continues teaching, now at the University of Central Florida, and researching areas such as environmental policy, economic development, and social services.

No ivory tower analyst, Glaser—like many urban faculty—has been out there in the community where the action is. In fact, hardly an area of the city has not been examined by the professor, ranging from groundwater contamination cleanup to use of the Wichita Public Library to funding for family planning, community child care needs, housing problems, the Parks and Recreation Department, government budgets, and personnel performance measures. "From the perspective of a professor," says Glaser, "my understanding of local governments has expanded rapidly resulting in unlimited classroom examples which illustrate the subject (research methods, performance measurement, policy evaluation, urban issues/policy)." In addition, Glaser says his interactive role with the university and the city has translated into numerous publication opportunities and has helped him formulate and organize policy content that must stand the test of implementation.

A listing of the number of urban faculty specialists who are "borrowed" for projects and positions in the urban megalopolis would be so extensive that it would be next to impossible to compose. Indeed, the contributions of these faculty to their metropolitan regions is so vast that most tourist information and economic development literature makes note of their presence and lists their availability among area assets. The days when cities once considered universities and their frequently rowdy students as little more than a community nuisance have long since disappeared.

PERFORMANCE EVALUATION

As the society changes and the concept of scholarship broadens, urban colleges and universities need to adopt more realistic and equitable approaches to their mechanisms for evaluating and rewarding faculty performance. *Metropolitan Universities* editor Ernest A. Lynton, who is professor at the University of Massachusetts, and Sandra E. Elman, assistant director of the Commission on Institutions of Higher Education at the New England Association of Schools and Colleges, discuss some of the new approaches to evaluation in a book they have written together. They cite the University of Louisville as an example of an urban institution that recognizes the demands made on its talented faculty and provides assurance that no one will be expected to be simultaneously involved in the entire spectrum of professional activities.[12] The university has established a process for continuing review of individual work loads for each faculty member. Faculty arrive at periodic reciprocal agreements with their dean or provost as to assignments and expectations. The goal is to develop such agreements with the clear understanding that they can be modified at subsequent reviews, depending on external needs, internal priorities, and personal circumstances. While this does not change the reward and status system in the larger higher-education community, its formal existence indicates that institutional rewards are changing.

The fact that the urban campus has become a major resource for the multiple communities it serves—that it is of the city, not simply in it— significantly expands the university's opportunities. Teaching and learning take place not just on campus but also in the larger arena of campus and community. In this light, on some campuses applied research is at least as important as basic research, and the transfer of knowledge from university to community becomes a prime component in institutional mission. In an address for the National Press Club's Morning Newsmaker program, former Cleveland State University president John A. Flower spoke of the challenge and excitement of universities becoming involved with the community:

> This is not a favorable situation for many in the academic world, especially some faculty who are not comfortable out in the marketplace, where politics and tense sociological issues become involved, distracting from the business of learning. Many prefer the Ivory Tower academic environment. . . . Some continue to say it is impossible to achieve the coupling of urban town and academic gown. The fact is that the necessity of effecting this synergism of cooperating is already upon us. That is why these [urban] campuses are the most vital, alive, and exciting places in America today.[13]

One urban institution that has led the way in this regard is George Mason University in Fairfax, Virginia. An article in *Virginia Business* describes how GMU in six short years attracted 60 full professors, "snatching some of them right from under the upstretched noses of Harvard, Princeton and MIT."[14] One of those recruits turned out to be Nobel Laureate James M. Buchanan, a professor of economics who developed theories about the economic forces that shape political decisions. Buchanan had not yet won the Nobel Prize when he was hired by GMU in 1983, but his Center for Study of Public Choice at Virginia Tech had gained considerable renown, and the professor was already coming to be known as a "rising star."

GMU had adopted the philosophy that to build a great university it must first recruit top-flight faculty. Bricks and mortar, it reasoned, would follow. GMU president Johnson noted that although it is difficult for a university that is not a household name to recruit academic superstars from prestigious universities such as Harvard or Yale, his campus had at least two major advantages. One was its location in an urban corridor of Northern Virginia, near Washington, DC. The other was its commitment to paying competitive salaries, spending better than 50 percent of its private support on endowed professorships and endowed chairs. Buchanan, however, who brought six other professors with him to GMU, said, "We were not attracted by financial reward. We actually lost out on some money."[15]

Besides its location and its commitment to faculty salaries, another factor that has attracted outstanding faculty to GMU is the university's flexibility and climate for innovation. As Johnson has put it, "We are not encumbered by the traditions and restrictions of the past." Faculty find the climate exciting and invigorating. Of his decision to join GMU, Buchanan said, "I was impressed with the dynamism of the place. It seemed to be on the go."[16]

Much of the innovative atmosphere that characterizes urban campuses is the natural result of their evolution from institutions which were established for the primary purpose of providing educational access at minimal cost for large numbers of place-bound taxpayers to colleges and universities that march to their own beat as interactive partners with the community. In their formative years, many of these institutions went about fulfilling that proscribed mission in several ways: (1) by limiting the curricula; (2) by placing heavy teaching responsibilities on full-time faculty; and (3) by hiring a substantial number of adjunct faculty. In the postwar years the influx of urban students was enormous. Generally, institutions grew rapidly, and demands for expanded curricula increased. New degrees continued to be added.

The mission to discover and promulgate knowledge broadened, but in many cases funding for urban campuses did not. Generally, urban campuses have operated with very limited resources, struggling to meet the educational needs of their students as well as those of the city. In a sense, these institutions were lean and mean before that phrase ever came to be the rallying cry of corporate America. The early and continued emphasis on undergraduate teaching and community service, coupled with a tendency to adopt the traditional research culture of their sister institutions in nonurban environments, placed enormous strains on both the financial and human resources of many campuses. Some—more than a few—have discovered, as Frank Newman puts it, that "No university ever moved to greatness by trying to be everything to everybody."[17] Yet many faculty were left feeling that just such an expectation existed for them.

Sandra Elman calls for the linking of the faculty reward system to the mission of the institution and suggests that the accreditation process is a means of ensuring that the faculty reward system is consistent with that mission.[18] It is important, Elman cautions, for faculty to know, at the time they are hired, precisely what types of scholarly activity are expected of them and how this and other professional activities will be evaluated and rewarded. It also is necessary for faculty to know that no one will be expected to engage in all types of professional activities. Contractual agreements, memoranda of understanding, or letters of communication between faculty members and contractors are as critical to the success of the evaluation process as is complete documentation of professional activities.

For all faculty, the need for research, both basic and applied, will continue to be a major activity of higher education, for as Drucker has pointed out, "the newest 'energy' of all—information—has no raw material or energy content at all" but is totally knowledge-intensive.[19] As mentioned earlier, however, the effective transmission of knowledge and its transfer to the society will become paramount. Just as capital investment was the key to prosperity in the past, education and competence are the forces that will produce progress now. With more than 75 percent of U.S. citizens living in or near the cities, urban higher education's prime mission will be to protect and promote the well-being of the nation through the education of its people. In this light, the role of faculty becomes critically important.

TEACHING AND DIVERSITY

If urban colleges and universities successfully fulfill their mission they will do so through faculty who are not only academically prepared but who also have developed the capacity to teach a student body that is incredibly diverse. Indiana University professor Eileen Bender points out that there is a growing tension between the expectations of today's college students and the traditional expectations of some faculty. While the essential values of the academy and its faculty have not changed—they are still the promulgation of literacy, critical thinking, historical and cultural awareness, and scientific inquiry—what has changed is the character of its student body and its bewilderingly diverse expectations. Says Bender:

> Faculty—always the essential convenors, conservators, and translators of undergraduate education—are feeling these pressures most keenly. While considerable attention is being given to the escalating research demands on the American professoriate, little attention has been focused on the escalating demands of teaching. This situation has been exacerbated by an expanding student-faculty 'expectation gap'.[20]

While it can be argued that the gulf between student and faculty expectations may not be nearly as pronounced on urban campuses as it is at traditional colleges and universities, it exists to some degree in all of public higher education. Many faculty on urban campuses were educated in traditional settings and came to the academy with fixed concepts based upon their own undergraduate context. Discovering that their students are, for the most part, independent, living off campus, and enrolled part-time is only the beginning of finding out who they are, what they need, what dreams and hopes they have, what their previous academic experience has been, and what life experiences have taught them. It is the enormity of student diversity that presents faculty with its greatest frustrations as well as challenges. The variations in cognitive development, learning style, cultural perception, language, and generational attitudes are both extraordinary and bewildering.

In a concept paper for the American Association of Community and Junior Colleges, Nelvia Brady, former chancellor of the City Colleges of Chicago, refers to the description of 1950s students in a book by Saul Bellow entitled *The Adventures of Augie March*:

> The students were children of immigrants from all parts, coming up from Hell's Kitchen, Little Sicily, the Black Belt, the mass of Polonia, the Jewish streets of Humboldt Park, put through the course of sifters of curriculum, and also bringing wisdom of their own. . . . [I]f you were going to prepare impoverished young folks for difficult functions, or if merely you were going to keep them out of trouble by having them read books, there were going to be some remarkable results begotten out of the mass. I knew a skinny, sickly Mexican too poor for socks and spotted and stained all over, body and clothes, who could crack any equation on the board; and also Bohunk wizards at the Greeks,

demon-brained physicists, historians bred under pushcarts, and many hard-grain poor boys who were going to starve and work themselves bitterly eight years or so to become doctors, engineers, scholars, and experts.[21]

Today, as Brady has pointed out, urban classrooms are no less exciting, and they are even more diverse. In the 1990s the walls are exceedingly porous. The impoverished, affluent, young, old, black, white, male, female, Asian, Hispanic, executive in mid-career, high school valedictorian—all of these and more mingle in the urban academy. Just as the demands on institutional support services have increased, so too have the demands on faculty.

For urban faculty the old presumptions about students as high school graduates with college preparatory backgrounds, children of alumni, financially supported by family, living in a dormitory, English-speaking, largely homogeneous in culture, to name a few descriptors, no longer exist. No givens, no common set of goals, values, academic prerequisites or aspirations exist. Traditional ground rules of teaching no longer apply. What works with one student is unsuccessful with others. Community that was once assumed must now be crafted.

Nancy Hoffman, director of Temple University's honors and interdisciplinary programs, notes that much of a useful nature has been written on learning styles and patterns of thought associated with race, class, ethnicity, or gender for the purpose of designing assignments and pedagogical practices that depart from the traditional thought of academia.[22] She points out that little has been written about the dynamics of today's classrooms and the stance or frame of mind of faculty as they stand in front of a class and assume the role of teacher. Today's classrooms, she says, "sometimes feel as if they are filled with charged particles repelling each other and in constant motion." Hoffman asks the questions many urban faculty face daily:

> How can we maintain the integrity of our own expert knowledge, yet model genuine openness to, and interest in, perspectives very different from our own? . . . How do we teach diverse students? But the question has to be rephrased, for the word 'diverse' used in this way implies that we—the teachers—are somehow a fixed center—the majority culture from which our minority students diverge or differ—when, in fact, we have no more claim to the center than they do. The question rephrased is: How do we acknowledge and incorporate into the learning community or classroom a variety of standpoints both

individual and group? If we hold a goal of constructing a community in the classroom, what are resources and techniques that are helpful?[23]

These questions and others equally important are not easily answered, but as urban campuses develop models for the "new university," so too do their faculties fashion new models for teaching and learning. In the process these institutions face the constant challenge of generating the capacity to teach an incredibly diverse mix of students and, at the same time, to educate those students both for the world of work and for the exercise of their civic duties in a global context. In this decade and in the century ahead—as the society is increasingly dominated and shaped by knowledge workers—those who teach assume a critical role. As Drucker and others have pointed out, education in and for the knowledge society will have a social purpose. In a society that has deciphered the genetic code, education cannot be value-free; the consequences are too frightening. The educated person must be equipped not just to earn a living but also to know how to live. If faculty are at the heart of academic enterprise, their teaching is the spark that lights the intellectual fires. If urban faculty are going to teach an increasing percentage of the society, their role as "fire lighters" becomes even more crucial.

Sam Crowell, an associate professor of elementary and bilingual education at California State University—San Bernardino, suggests that those who teach must change the way they view the world before they can find the best ways to prepare students for the future.[24] Writing of the usefulness of metaphors in facilitating the transition to new ways of thinking, he says, "For me, the concept of 'embeddedness' is a useful metaphor. For example, embedded in teaching is learning; the two cannot really be talked about separately. Embedded in the teacher is the student, for one is incomplete without the other. . . . Embedded in humans is nature; we are part of our environment, and it is part of us."[25]

FACULTY DEVELOPMENT

In this environment of challenge and change, the preparation of faculty takes on new and added significance. Can the historical monolith for university faculty development continue to be credible for the classrooms of the megalopolis? Some would answer that question by suggesting that multidisciplinary training is necessary for those who will teach an urban society. Others would disagree, suggesting increased specialization is required. G. Edward Schuh, dean of the Hubert H. Humphrey Institute of Public Affairs at the University of Minnesota, proposes new institutional arrangements that would enable campuses to offer multiple disciplinary capacities, including institutes or centers headed by faculty leaders "who can identify and conceptualize problems and who can meld together the various talents needed to solve these problems."[26] He calls for faculty in the coming years with a strong liberal arts background, followed by two to three years of specialization, and he further suggests the addition of a professional degree (an M.B.A., law degree, or a degree in public policy) followed by a Ph.D. for those interested in policy issues. Certainly, faculty of the future will need to receive the most comprehensive and up-to-date knowledge possible.

One of the most radical suggestions moves away from the single discipline base. Waetjen and Muffo suggest in a journal article the establishment of new academic units for interdisciplinary teaching and research related to urban affairs.[27] Such a unit would be structured with its own faculty core but in such a way as to provide for faculty from other colleges and departments to participate in its endeavors. The authors suggest that this involvement might take the form of leaves from the home department (within the same institution) in order to spend time in the interdisciplinary unit for work on a problem. The unit would provide a mechanism by which decisions regarding faculty promotion and tenure might be rendered. The length of time spent as a "visiting" faculty member participating in interdisciplinary activities of the unit—Waetjen and Muffo refer to it as "urban" but it could as easily bear some other designation—would depend on the nature of research, personal preferences of the faculty member, and the staffing situation of the home department or the new academic unit. Such "in and out" staffing within an institution, they suggest, would offer all faculty an opportunity to be involved in activities outside their own academic units.

To their credit, urban colleges and universities are generally believed to be more flexible than their sister institutions in considering the variety of combinations for academic preparation, teaching, research, contemplation, and continued learning. Such flexibility and willingness to deviate from tradition is particularly fortuitous in light of predicted faculty shortages that are expected to have a major impact on urban campuses in the decade ahead. Forecasts of these shortages surfaced as long as 15 to 18 years ago. More recently Howard R. Bowen and Jack H. Schuster predicted higher education will need 180,000 new faculty in the last half of the 1990s and an added 160,000 in the first four years of the new century.[28] These combined figures represent about 75 percent of the current full-time faculty nationwide. Another study, conducted in 1987 by William G.

Bowen and Julie Ann Sosa, looked specifically at doctorate-holding faculty in arts and sciences at four-year colleges and universities and concluded that more than half of the faculty at those institutions are likely to have departed by 2002.[29] A Mellon Foundation study projects that by 1997 there will be only seven applicants for every 10 faculty openings in the arts and sciences because the small crop of new Ph.D.'s will be dwarfed by the number of anticipated retirees.[30]

RECRUITMENT AND RETENTION

Those involved in higher education at the administrative level know all too well that the competition for faculty has already intensified, particularly for minority faculty. Institutional raiding, coupled with tightened resources for public institutions, intensifies the problem. Bowen and Sosa's study, which looks at the five types of institutions in the Carnegie classification, shows that the demand in the comprehensives category—within which most urban institutions fall—will be greatest in the latter years of this decade and in the early years of the twenty-first century. Results of the study indicate that urban institutions will have a bit more time to prepare than will other four-year colleges and universities, but "the demand among comprehensives will be highest just when all academic labor markets will be tightest."[31]

Projections such as these make it imperative that urban colleges and universities forge ahead in areas of faculty support and recruitment and in finding ways to enhance environments in which faculty teach and live. Fortunately, urban campuses offer faculty a number of attractions, among them these:

- more opportunities for applied research through business, industry, governmental, and social service connections;
- close proximity and easy access to state-of-the-art health care, major airports, extensive recreational and athletic activities, and cultural amenities such as museums, galleries, restaurants, live musical and stage productions, and so forth;
- greater opportunity for employment of other family members, a particularly significant factor for two-career families.

Despite these attractions, and others, however, urban colleges and universities must develop and implement strategies to prepare for future faculty shortages. These strategies might include, but are not exclusive to

(1) the recruitment of accomplished professionals already living in the area, including some who may have taken early retirements from business and industry; (2) the use of adjunct, visiting, and other nontenured faculty in positions that may lead to their eventual full-time employment; and (3) the grooming of future faculty by hiring those without terminal degrees and supporting them toward completion of their degrees.

No discussion of urban faculty would be complete without addressing the recruitment and retention of minority faculty, an even greater challenge. The problem is much too complex to address in a few simple paragraphs, but it is one that cannot be ignored. At least some "right track" initiatives in this regard are, I think, obvious, though some may not yield immediate results. Urban colleges and universities must (1) forge stronger community and public-school partnerships that will result in improved elementary and secondary education for minority youth; (2) improve the campus climate for minorities, both for minority faculty and students, and we must do this with *active* strategies that will build community and respect; (3) foster a campus environment that values teaching, mentoring, and collegial caring; and (4) not ignore the need for strategies that recognize and value cultural and social differences in our zeal to build community.

The number of studies on minority access and success indicates some progress, though not nearly enough (see Figure 4.1). Strides made in the 1960s and 1970s were positive. Indeed, U.S. Census Bureau statistics indicate that in the mid-1970s there was a brief period when black high school graduates were more likely to enroll on some campuses than their white counterparts. While that promise dimmed during the first half of the 1980s, recent figures are more encouraging. Between 1988 and 1990, total minority enrollment in U.S. colleges and universities increased 10 percent, doubling the rate of enrollment growth for all other groups in higher education.[32] For African American males, the increase was 7 percent, reversing a downward trend of the previous eight years.[33] Recent figures also indicate college matriculation rates for minorities also are increasing, at least at the undergraduate level.

Despite these encouraging figures, however, a 1990 research profile of opportunity structures in higher education in five metropolitan areas—Atlanta, Chicago, Houston, Los Angeles, and Philadelphia—showed that in all five regions, although whites made up a declining proportion of the high school graduates, they comprised an increasing proportion of high school graduates who went on to college.

Minorities Are Earning More Degrees

- In academic year 1988-89, 1,015,239 bachelor's degrees were awarded; 13 percent were earned by minorities.

- Between 1984-85 and 1988-89, the number of bachelor's degrees awarded to all minorities increased by 15 percent, from 112,988 to 130,081.

- Minorities earned 11 percent of all master's degrees in 1988-89, the same percentage as in 1986-87.

- In 1988-89, the largest proportion of master's degrees earned by minorities (27 percent) was in the field of education; however, between 1985 and 1989, the proportion of minorities earning degrees in this field declined by 41 percent. Between 1984-85 and 1988-89, the number of minorities earning master's degrees in business and management increased by 15 percent.

Degrees Awarded by Race and Ethnicity, 1988-89

Race/Ethnicity	Bachelor's	Master's	Doctorate
American Indian	4,046	1,133	84
Hispanic	29,800	7,270	625
Asian American	38,219	10,714	1,337
African American	58,016	14,076	1,071
White	858,186	241,607	24,895

FIGURE 4.1 Minority access and matriculation rates are improving following a slowdown during the first half of the 1980s.

Source: Cecilia A. Ottinger, ed., *Higher Education Today: Facts in Brief,* American Council on Education, 1992, 30; based on the *Tenth Annual Report on Minorities in Higher Education,* coauthored by Deborah Carter and Reginald Wilson for the American Council on Education.

Both Hispanic and black students, even though their high school graduation rates increased during the period of the urban study, failed to increase their opportunity at research, doctorate-granting, and comprehensive universities or at the liberal arts colleges, facts that have negative implications for all of higher education and for prospects of expanding the potential pool of minority faculty.[34]

Certainly, higher education has a critical role to play if minority access and matriculation rates in higher education are to be increased. Faculty must take the lead in improving undergraduate instruction for all and in incorporating race, class, gender, sexuality, and ethnicity as categories of scholarly methodology and examination. The task of enhancing participation of minorities at every level of higher education, however, belongs to all. Even though the process must, of necessity, be long-term, practical, short-term steps can be taken now. Del Mar College in Corpus Christi, Texas, has been able to improve its recruitment and retention of qualified faculty—particularly people of color—through an Academic Fellowship Program developed to augment the college's affirmative action efforts.[35] Del Mar seeks as fellows individuals who meet the educational requirements for teaching at community colleges but who have little or no classroom experience. Those selected as fellows serve as instructors for one year. When the program was started, Del Mar hired five fellows—two blacks, one Hispanic, one physically challenged person, and one female in a traditionally male department. In the fall of 1990 three more fellowships were filled. Two of those positions were filled by people of color, who subsequently became full-time faculty members. In the fall of 1991, eight fellowships were filled, with seven of the eight newly hired instructors being black or Hispanic.

Hiring, however, is not the end of Del Mar's efforts to build its minority faculty participation. Once they are employed, new fellows are assigned full-time faculty mentors who monitor and evaluate their progress, giving feedback on their strengths and weaknesses. When a full-time tenure track position is vacated, the academic fellows are given an opportunity to compete for openings on an equal footing. Former Houston high school math teacher Antonio Davis read an ad for the fellowship program in a Dallas newspaper. He applied, was accepted, and later was elected by students as "Instructor of the Year." The 26-year-old Davis said his goal is to earn a Ph.D. and to teach at the university level. Without the fellowship program, he said, his chances for doing that would have been slim.[36]

In the midst of negativities, it is important, I believe, to highlight successes such as those at Del Mar and to use them as examples of what all urban colleges and universities can do with commitment and cooperation of faculty and administration. Another positive example involving faculty is the San Diego Community College District, which initiated and managed "Project Success," a multi-year project for modifying patterns of student entry, testing, and placement. Arthur Cohen and Florence Brawer reported in their book on community colleges that "the activity itself was not unusual, but the faculty's conceiving and conducting it was a departure from typical practice."[37] The authors suggest that faculty can build on these kinds of involvement and take a lead in shaping curriculum, integrating academic support services with instruction, and measuring student learning on a college-wide basis.

What then can be said in summary about the asphalt intelligentsia? First, they, like faculty everywhere, are engaged with the responsibility for intellectual development and the advancement of knowledge. They teach, they inquire, and they serve. While the context and the challenges are almost always different from the setting in which they learned to be faculty, the richness and the possibilities of the urban campus make it an exciting and dynamic appointment. To believe that urban faculty are somehow inherently different from other university faculty is a misperception. To believe that they face more learning challenges, more diversity, and simultaneously more opportunity for innovation and inter-action is an accurate assumption. To call them the "asphalt intelligentsia" is more than a good "sound bite"; it is a very real description of their context and the nature of their work.

REFERENCES

1. John Naisbitt and Patricia Aburdene, *Megatrends 2000: Ten New Directions for the 1990s* (New York: Avon Books, 1990; reprint, New York: William Morrow, 1990), 6, 7 (page citations are to Avon edition).

2. Lindsay A. Desrochers and Don E. Detmer, "From the Ivory Tower to the Unisearchity," *Educational Record* (Fall 1990): 10.

3. Peter F. Drucker, *The New Realities* (New York: Harper & Row, 1989), 233, 247–50.

4. George D. Kuh et al., eds., *Involving Colleges* (San Francisco: Jossey-Bass, 1991).

5. Patricia R. Plante, "Form and Texture of a Professional Life," *Metropolitan Universities* 1 (Spring 1990): 58–65.

6. Ibid., 58.

7. Ibid., 65.

8. Kay Rogers, "The Art of Anticipation," *Indiana Alumni* (September/October 1991): 20–23.

9. Timothy Healy, commencement address, Virginia Commonwealth University, Richmond, VA, 18 May 1985.

10. Peter Szanton, *Not Well Advised* (New York: Russell Sage Foundation and the Ford Foundation, 1981), 21–22.

11. William C. Pendleton, "Urban Studies and the University—The Ford Foundation Experience" (speech delivered at New Orleans Regional Conference of the Office of Urban Affairs, 5 April 1974).

12. Ernest A. Lynton and Sandra A. Elman, *New Priorities for the University* (San Francisco: Jossey-Bass, 1987), 149.

13. Mary E. Skelly, "The Urban University Edge," *School and College* (May 1990): 8.

14. Karl Rhodes, "Talent Now, Buildings Later," *Virginia Business* (August 1989): 6.

15. Ibid., 7.

16. Ibid., 8.

17. Frank Newman, *Choosing Quality: Reducing Conflict between the State and the University* (report of the Education Commission of the States, Denver, 1987).

18. Sandra E. Elman, "The Faculty Reward System and Accreditation," *Metropolitan Universities* 1 (Spring 1991): 38–39.
19. Drucker, *The New Realities*, 123.
20. Eileen T. Bender, "Indiana University: Adjusting the Educational 'Fit,'" *Policy Perspectives* (Bloomington, IN: Indiana University, November 1991): 5B–6B.
21. Nelvia M. Brady, "The Larger Context of Urban Community College Finance" (report for the American Association of Community and Junior Colleges, April 1991).
22. Nancy Hoffman, "But Here and Now We Are Together," *Metropolitan Universities* 1 (Spring 1991): 56, 57.
23. Ibid., 57.
24. Sam Crowell, "A New Way of Thinking: The Challenge of the Future," *Educational Leadership* (September 1989): 60–62.
25. Ibid., 60–62.
26. G. Edward Schuh, "The Preparation of Future Faculty for Metropolitan Universities," *Metropolitan Universities* 1 (Spring 1991): 82.
27. Walter Waetjen and John A. Muffo, "The Urban University: Model for Actualization," *The Review of Higher Education* 6 (Spring 1983): 207–15.
28. Zelda F. Gamson, Dorothy E. Finnegan, and Ted I. K. Youn, "Assessing Faculty Shortages in Comprehensive Universities," *Metropolitan Universities* 1 (Spring 1991): 88.
29. Ibid.
30. Alan Deutschman, "Why Universities Are Shrinking," *Fortune* (24 September 1990): 73–75.
31. Gamson, Finnegan, and Youn, "Assessing Faculty Shortages in Comprehensive Universities," 91.
32. Cecilia A. Ottinger, ed., *Higher Education Today: Facts in Brief*, American Council on Education, February 1992, 31.
33. Ibid., 31.
34. Faith G. Paul, "Access to College in a Public Policy Environment Supporting Both Opportunity and Selectivity," *American Journal of Education* (August 1990): 351–88. First published by the University of Chicago, 1990.
35. "Fellowships Help Recruit Minority Faculty," *Community College Week* 25 November 1991, 7.
36. Ibid.
37. Arthur M. Cohen and Florence B. Brawer, *The American Community College* (San Francisco: Jossey-Bass, 1989), 371.

CHAPTER
five
❖ ❖ ❖ ❖ ❖ ❖

Urban Frustrations:
Perceptions and Realities

The difficulty of those in higher education in fully accepting the changes that a different population and a new social and economic profile have brought has caused the educational system as well as society to be slow in responding to obvious new needs that have emerged. In higher education the best response to the needs of New Majority learners has generally come from urban colleges and universities. Certainly, in many respects they have had no choice but to deal with the situation. In fact, students were at their doors ready to study in their classes almost before urban campuses realized something very new and different was happening. To imply that urban institutions immediately recognized and embraced the changed population would be inaccurate. Indeed, the predictable first-wave response to the new student body—characterized by more minorities, more women, more part-time and older students—was simply to define the group as an anomaly that required a few minor adjustments. Initially, the response amounted to adding some evening and weekend classes. The fact that these students were labeled "nontraditional" was a clear indication that in the beginning not even urban higher education viewed them in any way as the norm. It was not until they constituted a majority of the enrollees in higher education that the term nontraditional began to be discarded in favor of a more accurate description, "the New Majority."

PERCEPTIONS ABOUT THE NEW MAJORITY

Because any significant change is often perceived as a threat, some in the academy were quick to downplay the profile of the new student. "Nontraditional students" were characterized in various ways as "second-class":

They were often labeled as less serious about their studies, generally underprepared for college-level work, predominantly from "culturally deprived" populations, and economically disadvantaged, to name a few common perceptions. A number of highly publicized open-admissions failures in the 1960s served to reinforce these stereotyped and elitist attitudes and were cited by many faculty members and some colleges and universities as "proof" that this new kind of student was somehow inferior. The fact that students who could have been predicted to fail without some assistance—academic, financial, or otherwise—did fail after not receiving that assistance was used to support the notion that they really did not "belong."

In an article linking college access to public policy, Faith Paul asserts that public pressure for broad access to higher education following World War II spurred a number of policy initiatives that were in direct conflict with the egalitarian principles espoused through the Northwest Ordinance and later through the Hatch Act.[1] Among those she cites is the diversification of public higher education institutions, with different types of campuses established as preparation for different adult roles to be assumed. "This was consonant with the historical development of colleges and universities in America and represented a distinctly different approach from that adopted by American high schools when they changed from elite to mass institutions," says Paul. She also cites several other policies that served to undergird the notion of elitism, among them the authority of the state to assign a specific purpose to each campus in its public system—research, education for a Ph.D., comprehensive education, liberal arts education, or an education in two years—and the adoption of managed enrollment at the undergraduate level. Writes Paul:

> There was concern among important constituencies that a large enrollment could not possibly have the academic ability that had characterized the smaller group of students who had traditionally pursued higher education; therefore, some means was needed to generate access while protecting the quality of the higher education institutions. Dropout rates at the four-year campuses were already high, and there was an interest in protecting the state from funding education at the four-year level for students who were not capable of benefiting from it.[2]

At the same time these policies were being formulated, many states also established a comprehensive system of two-year colleges, designed to absorb large numbers of the new students who were clamoring at the gates of higher education. To their everlasting credit, it was these institutions—the junior and community colleges—that first embraced the New Majority populations and worked diligently to meet their needs. As they were doing so, however, many four-year institutions simultaneously raised their admissions standards. Paul cites the extreme example of the state of California, which mandated that access to the University of California campuses be predicated on ranking in the upper eighth of all high school graduates, that access to the California State colleges and universities be based on ranking in the upper third of all high school graduates, and that any student who fell below the top third of all high school graduates would have to enter higher education at the community college level. The idea was to create opportunity structures for all students who wanted to attend college in their home state. But most of the comprehensive colleges and many of the community and junior colleges were located in urban areas, and as flagship institutions began to accept only those who graduated at the very top of their high school classes, the idea that urban students were in some way inferior was again reinforced.

After a time, however, the successes of New Majority students were too obvious to be denied. Many of them graduated, earned postbaccalaureate degrees, established themselves in professional positions in the community, and came to be recognized among the states' important citizens. Of those colleges and universities who previously had been reluctant to open their doors to the New Majority, many began to rethink what they might have done, given the example of community colleges, to bring about such demonstrable intellectual development. Gradually, efforts to serve these students began to flourish, and the successes of urban campuses in educating New Majority students began to be reported nationwide.

The misperception of the New Majority student as scholastically "second class" is stubbornly persistent. That these students are stigmatized because they are more likely to be minority, poor, female, part-time, older, or require developmental course work at the outset of their academic program is grossly unfair. Moreover, the notion that they are not capable of intellectual achievement cannot be supported. From the ranks of one of the campuses I served have come Robert Rucker, the first African American judge to be named to Indiana's State Appellate Court; Congressman Peter Visclosky, who has been named one of the 10 brightest people in the U.S. House of Representatives; attorney Roy Dominguez, who heads Indiana's unemployment and workmen's compensation commission; and teacher Judith Lebryk, who was one of 53 outstanding high school teachers in the United States to be recognized at the White House. Data about the successes of New Majority students are abundant. One particularly noteworthy comparison is that in the last 20 years the City Colleges of New York have produced more Ph.D. candidates than have come from the ranks of the nation's Ivy League institutions, even though many Ivy League graduates are more likely to have had family financial support for postgraduate studies.

The persistent public perception that urban college and university students are somehow not quite as able as other students is as inaccurate as it is unfair, and, while individual anecdotal evidence to the contrary is readily available, statistical information, as noted earlier, is hard to come by. The information-gathering efforts of the Urban Student Affairs Data Exchange Network, of which my own institution is a member, is beginning to build a credible and valuable data base. Currently, the network is tracking graduation and retention rates of its members. Hopefully, more urban campuses will join this group, and we will begin to have available the kinds of statistical data needed to better serve students and to impact public policy positively with regard to funding for postsecondary institutions in urban settings.

PERCEPTIONS ABOUT URBAN FACULTY

To some degree urban faculty are misperceived and sometimes unfairly characterized as less than excellent. While it is fair to say that large numbers of faculty in urban institutions are energized by the diversity of their students and the importance of their work, they, too, often find themselves in scholarly settings where they are called upon to defend their reasons for choosing to stay at urban campuses. Former Carnegie Foundation fellow R. Eugene Rice, now vice president and dean of faculty at Antioch College, discusses the way in which faculty are stigmatized by their involvement with New Majority learners:

> It is somehow ironic that the programmatic areas that could provide new sources of institutional vitality over the next decade are precisely those areas where if faculty get involved, given the dominant professional model, they run the risk of being de-classed professionally. To become involved in programs for the adult learner, interdisciplinary studies, or, even, general education is to take on a kind of second class citizenship—to move toward the margins of the profession.[3]

The desire to emulate traditional models and the confusion over the roles and missions of emerging urban institutions brings frustration as well. Frank F. Wong, in a speech describing the comprehensive university as "the ugly duckling of higher education," recalls the faculty tensions he encountered when he first arrived at the University of the Redlands:

> A significant number of faculty wanted to pursue the Pomona prototype. A smaller number wished that we were more like Stanford where professional and graduate schools set the tone and dominate the budget. Still others wanted Redlands to be like Hampshire or Evergreen, overtly unconventional and self-consciously progressive. One did not have to look far for the source of the identity problem. There was no definitive model. . . . Because that species of institution is so poorly defined and ill understood, those of us at such universities need to create their meaning and interpret their significance.[4]

Only quite recently have urban campuses been successful in recruiting faculty from flagship institutions. This circumstance is a direct result of the erroneous perception that "the traditional model of the academy is more desirable" and an accompanying perception that "urban faculty somehow are not as scholarly or accomplished." When one reads the awards lists in higher education, faculty from urban institutions are almost always significantly represented among them. At the campus where I am now president, the founding dean of our internationally recognized College of Polymer Science and Polymer Engineering is a graduate of the university he now serves. A former chief scientist for the Air Force and director of the U.S. Air Force materials Laboratory at Wright-Patterson Air Force Base, Akron's Frank Kelley is a "hometown boy" who earned B.S., M.S., and Ph.D. degrees at the University of Akron and went on to distinguish himself both in industry and in the military before returning to his alma mater. That Dean Kelley returned to the University of Akron to teach, do research, and serve in a key administrative position is no more of an anomaly than the fact that there is a Nobel Prize winner on the faculty of George Mason University. That the Indiana University—Purdue University campus in Indianapolis was able to recruit 35 key faculty from other institutions in 1990–91, including Harvard, Michigan, Johns Hopkins, and Temple, was really no surprise. Each of these circumstances was as natural as it was predictable.

NEW EDUCATIONAL DEMANDS

Despite the fact that most faculty "thrive" on the diversity of students and the flexibility of urban campuses, many also admit they are challenged—sometimes even frustrated—by their own lack of preparation for this new environment. Unlike Frank Kelley, many faculty, urban and nonurban alike, spent their own undergraduate years, and often their graduate years as well, in traditional settings, as residents on campus, just being students. Few of them came to the university in multiple roles of parent, employee, community volunteer, church worker, and student. The transition from traditional student to teacher of New Majority students is sometimes difficult, though not impossible.

In an article on the needs of commuter students, Barbara Jacoby, director of the National Clearinghouse for Commuter Programs and author of the book *The Student as Commuter: Developing a Comprehensive Institutional Response*, discussed the problem:

> It may be difficult for some professors and administrators to accept what may seem to them to be a lesser academic commitment. Many of them have acquired from their own experience as students deeply rooted ideas about higher learning that may hinder their ability to respond to new circumstances. For that reason faculty sometimes shun assignments to an urban campus. And commuters, both of traditional age and older, continue to be thought of as apathetic or uninterested in campus life.[5]

Because their development, training, and experience provide them with little or no background from which to respond to a number of critical questions and concerns brought by these new and very different students, faculty sometimes face great difficulties in adjusting to the changing needs of an urban campus environment. The dilemmas they face are very real. What ways do they need to teach in order to facilitate and maximize learning for the serious student who, because of circumstances beyond his or her control, had to wait a year to complete the second class in a sequence; must spread degree requirements over 16 semesters; or brings an Asian culture to a literature course that is entirely western? How can the professor facilitate the integration of knowledge for students whose study for a degree may span an entire decade? Can the professoriate really assume that a collection of courses constitutes an education? How does one bring the student to develop a spirit of inquiry while the student is working full-time, parenting, and attending classes? Are motivation and learning, as colleges and universities have long insisted, the entire respon-sibility of the student? What can be done to provide New Majority students with the same kinds of rich informal learning experiences that traditional students derived from dormitory study groups and bull sessions?

Urban campus administrators and seasoned faculty are well aware of the intellectual abilities and the potential of their students. While they are taking care of everyday problems, such as accommodating students' cars, job schedules, day care for offspring, and a host of other special needs of the New Majority, most are frustrated about the lack of success in finding satisfactory responses to the intellectual needs of their students. Data from the American Council on Education tell us that minority enrollment at U.S. colleges and universities has been growing at twice the rate of nonminorities, that the number of students age 25 and older increased by 59 percent between 1974 and 1988, and that by 1991 women accounted for 55 percent of all college students.[6] Considering the numbers of New Majority students now enrolled and the fact that they constitute a growing percentage of the national student body, it seems surprising that actual educational delivery systems on many urban campuses have not changed in more fundamental ways. The organization into semesters, the division of learning segments by courses and credits, the biweekly lecture, the course as disseminator of information—all of the vestiges of traditional models of higher education—continue to be the norm. To be sure, there are experiments with technology, television and video instruction, clini-cal course work, industrial and work-site components, and satellite class-room linkages, but even collectively these methods are only beginnings. Urban campuses, if they are to be effective in meeting the needs of a changing student body, must continue to explore alternative methods of educational delivery.

The reasons urban institutions are only just beginning to engage in substantial and fundamental rethinking of their structural mechanisms for educational delivery are numerous. The most pragmatic of those reasons probably lies in the fact that thus far urban colleges and universities have managed to move a great number of students to their educational goals without having to make dramatic changes. Too often, urban and nonurban campuses alike subscribe to the philosophy that if doing business in the usual way results in a large number of students meeting the end objectives, then that way must be adequate. Troubling retention numbers and low graduation rates of New Majority students, however, are an increasing cause for concern.

A second reason urban schools have been slow and reluctant to change is the lack of research and development into new methods of educational delivery. Urban faculty work loads are often quite heavy, leaving little time for exploration of new and more effective methods of teaching. Financial considerations are a key factor as well. Many public universities in urban settings are only modestly funded for teaching and research and are seldom, if ever, funded to experiment with educational change. Moreover, public budgets are generally enrollment-driven, and in a time of shrinking resources justification for time away from teaching—even for the discovery of ways to enhance learning—is very difficult to schedule. Additionally, foundations, and even public funds such as those dedicated to the improvement of postsecondary education, have shown little interest in support of such basic development projects.

An additional frustration of faculty involves knowing exactly how to make appropriate changes. Most of those who come to the academy are well trained, but generally in fields of narrow specialization. The preparation of a scholar is highly demanding, requires intense focus, and is a process that places predominant value on the mastery of a specific discipline. For such preparation to include instructional design, learning theory, adult development, or even basic institutional organization is nonexistent. Indeed, nearly every college faculty member is prepared in a monolithic design that includes lectures, exams, research, and publication. Many have had little or no teaching experience prior to their first university appointment. While they are, for the most part, exceptionally well prepared to advance the knowledge of their specific field, none can realistically be expected to arrive at the academy equipped to engage in issues of institutional change, methods of instructional delivery, or fundamental ways of advancing intellectual development. This is not to say they could not become prepared, or even that they would resist such learning; it is simply an acknowledgement that few, if any, professors have a background on which to draw for such bold and complex ventures.

Another reason urban campuses have made little progress in developing new methods of educational delivery lies in the academy's historical view of scholarship. This view places considerable value on the discovery of knowledge, less on its integration and application, and often the least value on its transfer through teaching. Rice, in an article discussing these aspects of scholarship, concludes that teaching "has far too long been implicit, unacknowledged, and virtually unnamed."[7] He refers to teaching as "a missing paradigm," noting that faculty often see scholarship and teaching as antithetical, competing for time and attention. While not dismissing the importance of knowledge discovery, Rice challenges the existing hierarchical arrangement that places predominant value on the acquisition of knowledge, which he terms "a status system that is firmly fixed in the consciousness of the present faculty and the academy's organizational policies and practices." He says:

> What is being called for is a broader, more open field, where these different forms of scholarship can interact, inform, and enrich one another. . . . Awareness that the dominant form of scholarship is inappropriate and counterproductive for the majority of our faculty, as well as our institutions, is widespread. The concern runs deep, yet when individual faculty are rewarded and "emerging" institutions launch drives toward higher standards of academic excellence, the older, narrow definition of scholarship as research is reasserted and given priority.[8]

One note of encouragement has been the establishment of the journal, *Metropolitan Universities*, whose goals are to provide a vehicle for recognizing high-quality efforts on emerging urban campuses and thus to bring them into the literature with the kind of recognition that refereed publications provide. It is a noteworthy and important step that was led by President Emeritus Paige Mulhollan of Wright State University in Dayton, Ohio.

Despite the preponderance of barriers to innovation in teaching-learning strategies, however, many individual faculty have found ways to adjust and accommodate New Majority students within the traditional framework. Some of those efforts were detailed in chapter 3. Other examples of faculty who have ventured into pioneering programs in an effort to spark student interest and stimulate intellectual engagement also exist. For example, at Cleveland State University, Professor of Anthropology John E. Blank worked with a colleague to create an interactive videodisk of images of normal and pathological human and primate skeletons to use in teaching anatomy.[9] The disk, used in laboratory courses, includes more than 21,000 color images of skeletons and 28 minutes of video images showing human movement. Blank explains that most anthropology laboratories have only a small number of human skeletons and fiberglass casts of human and primate skeletons, and a small sample of human fossil casts. The disk, with 462 human, 47 primate, and 387 fossil specimens, puts a well-equipped skeletal laboratory at the fingertips of Cleveland State students. Other examples of faculty innovation abound, and, despite the limitations already discussed, potentially fruitful interchanges about creative reorganization and new approaches to teaching are heard more frequently these days as institutional exploration of multiple delivery systems goes forward. While change undoubtedly will continue at a slow evolutionary pace, one can hope for speedier development, knowing that, for the most part, urban faculty and students have a shared goal of academic success.

OUTDATED STANDARDS

In discussing frustrations faced by urban campuses, some of the most serious difficulties are the ways in which approval, control, and governing bodies have been slow to recognize New Majority students and the New Majority timetable. One would naturally assume that important agents of the academy would be well informed about the dimensions of urban populations, the differences between today's student bodies and yesterday's, as well as the variety and depth of their needs. The actions of some approval-control agents suggest their knowledge and understanding in these areas is quite limited. For example, does taking more than five years to complete the degree program indicate the student has been dilatory or that the university has been excessively demanding? The answer to that question, of course, is no. Yet graduation and retention rates continue to be published, rewarded, and penalized, based on norms that are descriptive of an entirely different student population. Moreover, these kinds of artificial time frames fail to recognize that education increasingly is a lifelong process, that there is not an end date, and that on the most common-sense level, it is reasonable for educators to base their approach on an expectation of varying stages and levels of achievement at different points in time and over many years.

Former City Colleges of Chicago chancellor Nelvia Brady notes that urban campuses are regarded as critical to the mission of serving the highly varied needs of metropolitan populations, yet often are accused of being unfocused and inefficient because of the wide range of programs and offerings they develop in response to those needs. Brady, who chaired the Commission on Urban Community Colleges for the American Association of Community and Junior Colleges, goes on to say:

> [W]e are criticized when these [New Majority] students do not act or perform in accord with "traditional" collegiate expectations; when they "stop out," or even when they leave in good standing having

achieved a short-term goal. There is even criticism when students after several years successfully attain a degree. At the City Colleges of Chicago we recently completed a study which showed that 60 percent of our graduates take five years or more to receive what is nominally a two-year degree. We found that three-quarters mix part-time and full-time study, a strong majority do not enroll continuously. This demonstrates the impressive dedication of these students to their education. Yet Chicago opinion-makers interviewed by a consultant were dissatisfied rather than impressed; they regarded the time for degree completion as "unacceptably long."[10]

Related though somewhat different perceptions—and ones that are equally frustrating—in effect say that those who do not learn quickly do not belong in a college or university and that dropouts, stop outs, and failures can be taken as evidence that "high" standards are being maintained. Such assumptions fail to consider the institution's own inadequacies or mitigating circumstances that may cause students to leave the university. They also ignore the fact that at many urban campuses, particularly those which define themselves as comprehensive, only those in the top half of their high school graduating class or those who score above selected cutoff points on admissions exams are allowed entry in the first place. This fuzzy viewpoint accepts the notion that limiting access and graduating fewer students is a positive achievement because it somehow guarantees quality. In a knowledge-based economy, where the society can only flourish if large numbers of its citizens are educated, such a perception is one the nation can ill afford.

As American Council on Education senior scholar Reginald Wilson has pointed out, the academy's acceptance of social Darwinism, the belief that the purpose of higher education is to "weed out" students rather than to nurture them, is one of the reasons for the dismal record in educating Hispanics and African Americans, even while the numbers of potential students in these groups is increasing in the general population.[11] Wilson cites author James Coleman, who argues that schools often do little to encourage students' attainment and that they assume the best predictor of college success is parental income. He insists that expectations of student *capabilities* must change, that educators must be convinced that minority students *can* succeed in the university if, indeed, they are to do so. In fact, the same can be said for all New Majority learners.

ACCREDITATION

Another troubling area for urban colleges and universities is accredita-tion. While there is little dispute about the value of external evaluation of campus programs, many existing accrediting bodies bring as their only yardstick for excellence a model of education that was developed for a traditional, full-time, adolescent student. To apply what may be infinitely sensible provisions for that type of student population to students on urban campuses often results in totally defenseless (and useless) demands on an institution whose student population is comprised primarily of adults who are enrolled part-time. At times, the accreditation demands are so stringent that the institution is forced either to develop a program that is sound and reasonable for the population or become accredited by developing a program that meets the evaluating agency's requirements but is less effective in meeting the intellectual needs of its students. Ernest Boyer of the Carnegie Foundation for the Advancement of Teaching addresses the problem in a Carnegie Foundation report:

> In reality . . . there is still a tendency for visiting teams to judge colleges and universities quite conservatively, using traditional norms that inhibit innovations and restrict the full range of scholarly en-deavors. Especially disturbing is the way professional accrediting associations dictate detailed regulations and, in the process, violate the integrity of the campus[,] pushing institutions toward conformity. If the potential of American higher education is to be fully recog-nized, standards must be flexible and creative. Campuses should be encouraged to pursue their own distinctive missions, and innovation should be rewarded, not restricted.[12]

Institutional responses to the unfortunate realities of accreditation vary. Two of the most dramatic reactions are simply not electing to associate with the national or regional accrediting groups, or, as an alternative, working with other institutions to develop groups that pro-vide valid assessment and feedback more suitable for the actual population being served. An example of the second alternative is the fact that an entirely new national accrediting body—the Association of Collegiate Business Schools and Programs—was recently established to evaluate collegiate schools of business. On the positive side of the issue, not all accrediting bodies have provided such frustration, and some certainly have done all that could be asked in making certain that evaluations are sensibly administered and are helpful to the populations being served.

FUNDING

Formulas and models other than those imposed by accrediting bodies also are a major source of frustration for campuses with large New Majority enrollments. Among the most pernicious of these is the commonly employed funding measure of full-time equivalency, FTE. For whatever use this calculation of a "full-time equivalent" student is employed, the situations it creates often border on the absurd. As an example, one urban university chancellor tells that he was "scientifically" assigned resources for parking spaces for only a few more than half the number of cars driven by students who arrived each evening for classes on his campus. Parking funding in his state is based on FTE, with no allowance for the fact that the formula does not take into account a large enrollment of part-time students that cannot be accommodated each day.

The FTE as an index creates endless other unrealistic and frustrating situations. If, for example, FTE indicates there are 10,000 students who require counseling, instruction, water fountains, or whatever, on an urban campus this almost always means there actually are several thousand more students being served on campus. If a counselor is available on an FTE basis but students are attending on a part-time basis, the counselor may actually have up to four or five actual persons to assist for each student for which the campus is funded by the formula. The convenience and simplicity of such formulas for those whose job it is to apportion funding results in major inequities and unrealistic expectations.

California State University's Desdemona Cardoza spoke on this subject during a 1991 urban higher education conference at Cleveland State in 1991, noting that California State University—Los Angeles is funded at about the same FTE level as California State University—Chico, a nonurban campus in northern California, which serves approximately 14,400 students.[13] California State University—Los Angeles in the fall of 1990 was funded for 14,500 FTE students, even though it actually had almost 21,000 students on the campus using the library, using the restrooms, and moving through the campus all year long, daily and on weekends. An assistant vice president for information resources management, Cardoza said the end result of FTE funding is a system that discriminates against women, against students who rely on financial aid, returning older students, and part-time students. Insisting that this method of funding ensures that the promise of quality in higher education will remain unfulfilled for many of urban students, Cardoza read the following comments from an accreditation report of the Western Association of Schools and Colleges:

> [I]t is necessary to know the irony of a system that presses toward the inclusion of educationally disadvantaged students but distributes funds as if all students were traditional, full-time, well-prepared, native English-speaking, high school graduates. CSULA is constrained in its ability to serve its students by that fact. If California is what much of the nation will be in the next century, then CSULA is now what much of California higher education will be even sooner. Its success is of more than local importance, and that needs to be recognized in ways that matter.[14]

Such examples illustrate only a few of the ways in which the FTE index fails to fit the collegiate enterprise in sensible ways. Virtually every funding agency and urban campus can cite a quirk of some kind that demonstrates the continued lack of recognition that urban campuses and their populations are different from traditional models. The distinctions from traditional categories noted in chapter 2 become especially clear when traditional formulas are applied, nearly always with nonsensical results. Consider, for example, that some states have constructed academic facilities to accommodate large numbers of commuting students but prohibit the use of public dollars to build parking lots. And consider the fact that some states provide public funds for collegiate athletic facilities but prohibit the use of public funds for campus child-care facilities. At least one state appropriates millions of dollars for student financial aid but disqualifies all part-time students from eligibility. It is particularly ironic that such a rule should be adopted since part-time students most often are working, and, therefore, paying taxes which help finance the very financial aid funds for which they have been declared ineligible. The rationale used to justify such a decision is, on the face of it, just short of ludicrous: Full-time students are deemed eligible for financial aid because they are working harder at getting an education.

Lawrence Gold, president of Public Policy Advocates, Inc., in Washington, DC, notes that it makes no sense to narrow access to higher education when the *Workforce 2000* study tells us that by the turn of the century the mean years of education required for employment will rise to 13.5, and only 27 percent of all jobs will be in low-skilled occupations.[15] Too often, he adds, federal laws and regulations place obstacles in the path of adults—particularly at-risk adults—who might turn to college for their education and training. Says Gold:

Sometimes the obstacles are unintended; other times they may serve a program purpose, but turn a blind eye on the educational impact. Many of these obstacles have a chilling effect on adult college attendance and could be removed without significantly damaging other policy interests. . . . The new welfare reform act makes postsecondary education an "allowable" training activity that the state may approve on a case-by-case basis. However it is a rare state and a rare welfare office that will permit someone to receive welfare benefits while attending college—despite the fact that college graduates virtually never wind up back on welfare.[16]

Gold uses several examples to illustrate the ways federal policies make it difficult to go to college. Among them is that of a married women with three children, who works full-time and takes nine credits a term toward a B.A. degree during evenings when her husband is home. Together, the husband and wife earn $28,000, and she is halfway through her degree program. Then the couple divorces. The woman needs to earn more money and takes a second job at night. As a result, she must drop her course load to three credits a term and therefore is ineligible for full financial aid. Obviously, these regulations need to be made more flexible if we are to encourage people to participate in higher education with the expectation that they will build a better life for themselves and for their children.

Funding formulas and regulations are only a part of the problem. A significant frustration also exists as the result of the inability of many urban campuses to extend their academic programs and degree offerings. It is, in fact, not at all uncommon for urban campuses to wait literally years to add degrees that are being requested and are needed by the populations they serve. If students are available to pursue such programs and campuses are interested in providing them, why the wait? The answer, again, rests with perception. Faced with a revenue base that is not expanding and high school graduation rates that are flat, many states are unwilling to approve additional degree programs. This reluctance is based on their perception that the number of college-goers is declining, when in reality the number in urban areas is increasing. A second erroneous perception is that if a degree or program is available at another location, then duplication is not warranted. From the viewpoint of place-bound students, however, if the needed degree is available even as close as 100 miles away, it may just as well be offered on the moon for all the good it will do them.

Funding cuts for higher education are having a major impact on many urban campuses (see Figures 5.1 and 5.2). *Chronicle of Higher Education*

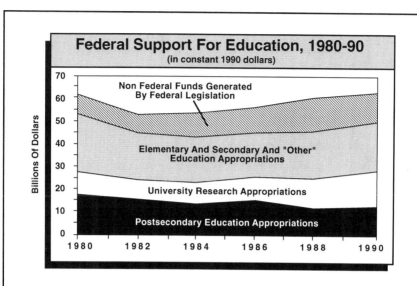

FIGURE 5.1 Federal appropriations for postsecondary education, exclusive of funds for research, fell during the 1980s from $17 billion to $12 billion in constant dollars. Funding constraints hit urban institutions particularly hard.

Source: Cecilia A. Ottinger, ed., *Higher Education Today: Facts in Brief,* American Council on Education, 1992, 46; based on *Federal Support for Education: Fiscal Years 1980 to 1990,* published by U.S. Department of Education, National Center for Education Statistics.

reporter Goldie Blumenstyk writes that at Wayne State University the inability of Detroit to overhaul a municipal lighting system led to streetlight outages around the campus. In New York City, funding for CUNY's seven community colleges dropped from $122 million in 1989–90 to $76.6 million in 1990–91, at the same time enrollments at those colleges increased by more than 5,700 to 67,000. At the Community College of Philadelphia the portion of its budget that comes from city funding dropped from 38 to 24 percent, and the situation would have been worse except for the fact that the college president, Ronald J. Temple, led 1,000 students, faculty, and staff on a march and rally at City Hall in protest. The protest worked. The next day Philadelphia's mayor pledged additional support, and ultimately, the college received an extra $500,000 from the city. But it was the first increase in six years.[17]

In Florida, Miami-Dade Community College trustees announced they would seek approval of a one million two-year property tax levy that would produce a $130 million "community endowment," marking the first time that M-DCC had gone to the local voters for help in its more than three decades' history.[18] President Robert McCabe cited deteriorating state

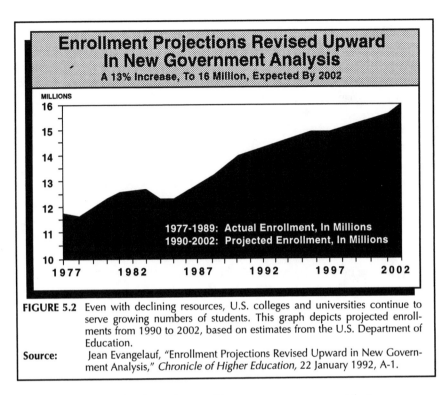

FIGURE 5.2 Even with declining resources, U.S. colleges and universities continue to serve growing numbers of students. This graph depicts projected enrollments from 1990 to 2002, based on estimates from the U.S. Department of Education.

Source: Jean Evangelauf, "Enrollment Projections Revised Upward in New Government Analysis," *Chronicle of Higher Education,* 22 January 1992, A-1.

support that cut funding drastically in recent years, with income per student from the state sliding 16 percent between 1989 and 1990 while the college was expected to serve 22 percent more students. For the first time ever, Miami-Dade was forced to curtail enrollment in 1991–92, cutting its student enrollment for the winter term by 3,000 students. These actions came at a time when economic downturn in the Miami area, precipitated by the failure of several major financial institutions and the demise of Miami-based Eastern and Pan American airlines, created a rising demand for college programs.

DEVELOPMENT ISSUES

Clearly, misperceptions about the realities of urban higher education continue to affect the majority of college-goers negatively. Legislative mandates and bureaucratic formulas, however, are only the beginning of the problem. Often, the "hyphenated campuses" in particular find that major university donors are encouraged to channel their donations for the embellishment of traditional, more richly appointed campuses while urban institutions operate in spartan surroundings with few amenities to make campus life more comfortable for commuting students. The erroneous notion is often presented that the more traditional campuses provide a better return on the investment since it is assumed, incorrectly, that more students are likely to be served in traditional settings.

One administrator tells a story of his days as a community college president on a campus that admitted students with quite limited educational backgrounds and almost routinely managed to bring them to remarkable academic achievement levels. Indeed, the intellectual progress of students on the campus was a matter of great pride. On one occasion the president met with some friends from his former institution, which was well known and was quite selective in admitting to its student ranks only those who were top-level achievers but whose graduation rates for those students was not at all remarkable. His former colleagues inquired whether he missed being at a "good" college. Until "good" is no longer used as a synonym for traditional university models, many excellent institutions providing quality education to thousands of students will continue to face the frustrations of common misperceptions.

LACK OF SUPPORT

A final category of frustration for urban campuses centers around their ability, or lack of it, to garner the kind of emotional support that translates itself into major donors, supportive alumni and friends, community value, and pride. While football teams, marching bands, and spacious conference facilities do not form the core of an academic enterprise, they invariably bring the institution special recognition while building pride and creating the perception that the campus is of great value to the community. A local team inspires bonding—community unity, spirit, even revenues—and can bring loyalists to campuses in ways that are as predictable as they are amazing. Unfortunately, many urban campuses simply do not have or cannot justify funds for such activities. For those who have justified expenditures for activities such as sports, the results have been enormously positive. The University of Central Florida, whose football team is a relatively recent addition to the campus, has reported attendance of 25,000 fans per game, whether the team was winning or not.

The lack of bond-building amenities is certainly not at the top of the list of urban university frustrations, but it is a real problem. Because urban colleges and universities are centered in large population centers, the more people who come to associate with these campuses, the more support they are likely to receive. Those who donate time and financial resources, who lobby, volunteer, or even encourage others to enroll at the campus, not only assist in its development but also help explode the myths and overcome the misperceptions. Fortunately, many myths are beginning to give way as community leaders recognize the importance of urban institutions in the intellectual, social, and economic life of their cities. In an article highlighting the growth of the University of Alabama—Birmingham and other colleges and universities in metropolitan areas of the South, the *New York Times* notes that these institutions have brought the classrooms to population centers, eliminating travel and boarding from the cost of higher education, preparing an educated citizenry, and stimulating economic development.

Karen De Witt writes:

> It seems a simple truth, but the concept that education dollars ought to be spent where people live seemed hard to grasp for Southern legislators, who were attuned to spending their higher education budgets mainly in towns like Tuscaloosa (Ala.), Oxford, Miss., and Athens, Ga. When money and students began to flow into the new urban universities, it changed not only local economies but also the educational pecking order within many state university systems. That local business leaders recognize the benefits of the university is evident, however, in a recent capital fund-raising drive. Some of the city's top corporate executives led it and helped raise $67 million.[19]

TERRITORIALITY

Chief among their frustrations is the difficulty urban campuses encounter in attempting to expand the range of academic opportunities available to students. Since many urban colleges and universities have not been able to offer the full array of programs and degrees their students need, leaders of urban institutions, on a rather regular basis, appear before coordinating councils or regents seeking—and in some instances almost begging for—permission to add programs. While all campuses generally face at least some opposition in such instances, for many urban institutions the opposition is heightened, in part because of territorial and competitive concerns. Often, in fact, urban campuses are denied approval of badly needed degree programs simply because another institution perceives the request as a threat to its own academic viability.

As a hypothetical example, a nearby liberal arts college with a student body recruited nationally may object to new degrees at an urban university on the basis that the addition of these degrees would compete with its existing programs. If that is the case, it is a fair and reasonable issue. More often than not, however, the objection is unfounded since the two institutions very likely serve entirely different student populations, with the liberal arts college drawing students from throughout the country while the urban campus focuses almost entirely on students who live in the immediate area. As excellent as the small liberal arts undergraduate college model is, no urban campus I know of is trying to develop along those lines of an undergraduate college. Nor are many urban campuses recruiting nationally, although a few of the large campuses do. Generally, both the fear of the nearby traditionally modeled campus and the frustration of the urban institution could be avoided through an understanding that the urban goal is not to diminish the sister institution, but only to find ways to meet the increasing needs of its students and its communities. In some cases such understanding has been accomplished, with public urban campuses working closely with other area institutions to ensure that each is supporting the other and is noncompetitive. In those cases, libraries, faculties, advanced classes, and even degree programs are shared. Such a reinforcing environment creates a "win-win" situation, not simply for the institutions but for their students, whose needs are being met.

Similar fears related to urban growth can sometimes be found at flagship campuses where, again, the assumption is that if nonflagship campuses grow and expand their academic program offerings, then somehow the "mother" campus will be diminished. While some students, who make heroic sacrifices to move away from home for a flagship campus degree, would enroll at an urban campus if that degree were available closer to home, it is highly unlikely that the number of these students is substantial. In most cases, the fear is groundless. No flagship campus in the nation has an entire catalogue of exclusive degree offerings, and they all seem to be prospering. Indeed, most admissions offices try to counsel students to enroll at the institution that provides the best fit for their academic goals. A clearer understanding of the nature and role of urban colleges and universities would go a long way toward eliminating the perception that they are a formidable threat and would greatly enhance the potential for beneficial cooperative ventures between urban and nonurban campuses.

Boyer calls for the kind of diversity in higher education that would build a "true community of learning." He writes:

> [L]et's have great research centers where undergraduate instruction *also* will be honored. Let's have campuses where the scholarship of

teaching is a central mission. Let's have colleges and universities that promote integrative studies as an exciting mission through a core curriculum, through interdisciplinary seminars, and through team teaching. And let's also have colleges and universities that give top priority to the scholarship of application, institutions that relate learning to real life—in schools, in hospitals, in industry, and in business. . . . What we are calling for is diversity with dignity in American higher education—a national network . . . in which each college and university takes pride in its own distinctive mission and seeks to complement rather than imitate the others.[20]

As the myths fade and the role of urban campuses is more fully understood, the desired goal is that state and city fathers, funding agencies, accrediting bodies, and others will recognize the urgency of the urban higher education mission. Persistent and erroneous notions about the quality of urban institutions, the significance, numbers, and diverse nature of New Majority students are cause for serious concern. So long as these misperceptions impose limits on urban colleges and universities, the nation's opportunity to bring growing numbers of its citizens into the social and economic mainstream will be diminished. The challenge is to create a climate in which the realities of urban America are clearly and indelibly etched in the nation's consciousness. Only then will appropriate levels of resources for educational delivery be channeled to the institutions that serve most of the residents of the United States.

REFERENCES

1. Faith G. Paul, "Access to College in a Public Policy Environment Supporting Both Opportunity and Selectivity," *American Journal of Education* (August 1990): 352–54. First published by the University of Chicago, 1990.
2. Ibid., 353.
3. R. Eugene Rice, *Faculty Lives: Vitality and Change* (Saint Paul, MN: Northwest Area Foundation Report, 1985), 45.
4. Ernest L. Boyer, *Scholarship Reconsidered: Priorities of the Professoriate* (Princeton, NJ: The Carnegie Foundation for the Advancement of Teaching, 1990), 62.
5. Barbara Jacoby, "Adapting the Institution to Meet the Needs of Commuter Students," *Metropolitan Universities* 1 (Summer 1990): 65.
6. Cecilia A. Ottinger, ed., *Higher Education Today: Facts in Brief*, American Council on Education, February 1992, 30, 57, 65.

7. R. Eugene Rice, "The New American Scholars: Scholarship and the Purposes of the University," *Metropolitan Universities* 1 (Spring 1991): 7–18.

8. Ibid., 15–16.

9. Beverly T. Watkins, "Technology Update," *Chronicle of Higher Education*, 22 January 1992, A-23.

10. Nelvia M. Brady, "The Larger Context of Urban Community College Finance" (concept paper for the American Association of Community and Junior Colleges, 14 April 1991), 4.

11. Reginald Wilson, "Enhancing Minority Attainment: A Multicultural Perspective in Higher Education" (address at a Conference on Minorities in Higher Education, Indiana University—Kokomo, 17 September 1991).

12. Boyer, *Scholarship Reconsidered*, 79–80.

13. Desdemona Cardoza, "Advancing Urban Higher Education: The California State University System" (presentation at the National Conference on Urban Higher Education, Cleveland State University, 7 October 1991).

14. Ibid.

15. Lawrence N. Gold, "Educating At-Risk Adults: Success Means Breaking Down Federal Policy Barriers," *Change* (July/August 1990): 6.

16. Ibid., 7.

17. Goldie Blumenstyk, "City Budget Cuts Take Another Toll on the Nation's Urban Institutions," *Chronicle of Higher Education* 4 December 1991, A-38.

18. Maurice D. Weidenthal, ed., "Miami-Dade Takes Its Case to the Voters," *Urban Community Colleges Report* 2 (January 1991): 1, 4.

19. Karen De Witt, "Universities Become Full Partners to Cities in South," *New York Times*, 13 August 1991, A-12.

20. Boyer, *Scholarship Reconsidered*, 64.

CHAPTER
six
❖ ❖ ❖ ❖ ❖ ❖ ❖ ❖

Urban Linkages:
High Rise, High Stakes,
and High Hopes

The traditional challenge of American higher education has been to search for truth and knowledge and to transfer to society processes we define as teaching, research, and service. At the same time, colleges and universities also have embraced the broad mission of educating people for the fulfillment of social, civic, and professional responsibilities. Given the magnitude of those goals, and despite higher education's oft-publicized inadequacies and shortcomings, I would argue that we really have done a very good job. In aspiring to bring higher education to all people, we have undertaken what no other nation in history has dared to attempt, and we have done so with an amazing degree of success.

In 1940, less than one American adult in 20 (4.6 percent) was a college graduate, but by 1986 the number had quadrupled to one in five (19.4 percent), and by the late 1980s the percentage of adults with college degrees was higher than the percentage with high school diplomas in 1930.[1] Between 1976 and 1981, the salary of the average recent college graduate rose 25 percent faster than inflation, and the earnings advantage of college-educated young adults grew even greater between 1978 and 1987.[2] But statistics (which reveal both success and failure, depending on interpretation) do not tell the whole story. Positive changes in resources and in the quality of life both for individuals and for the society are a more accurate reflection of the nation's educational accomplishments. Without underestimating the immense problems the United States faces today, some positives are these:

- The U. S. today produces 25 percent of the world's industrial output but still has only 5 percent of the world's population.

- The U. S. produces 25 percent of the world's gross national product— more than Japan and the Soviet Union (number two and number three) combined.
- During the 1990s well-educated, skilled U.S. information workers will earn the highest wages in history.
- Between 1969 and 1986 the percentage of families classified as "lower class" and as "middle class" shrank as more and more families, both black and white, moved into the upper-middle income ranks.
- Between 1959 and 1986 the percentage of Americans living in poverty fell from 22.4 percent to 13.5 percent.
- Today, 50 percent of all adults receive at least some college education, compared with 25 percent of all adults in the 1950s.
- Among those households earning $75,000 or more per year, 66 percent of the heads of households are college graduates.[3]

Most urban colleges and universities, which evolved during the post-World War II period when the United States made such great social and economic strides, have played a key role in moving the society forward, not simply in terms of educating large numbers of citizens but also in forging critical developmental partnerships in several key areas: business and industry, government and human services, and public education. As we move through this decade and into the twenty-first century, the challenges of knowledge discovery and transfer, though still important, are not enough. Their location gives urban colleges and universities an even broader mission than their sister institutions, where for multiple reasons service has been limited and the focus has traditionally centered on basic research and teaching to a select group of learners. The metropolitan society presents a vast array of problems and issues that require the best our institutions of higher education have to offer. The responses of urban campuses may be catalogued as teaching, research, or service. And, while the labels are unimportant, the responses are essential

PARTNERSHIPS WITH BUSINESS AND INDUSTRY

Declaring that "the critical mass of today's urban state university is the critical mass of its community," former Cleveland State University president John A. Flower has called on urban campuses to continue efforts that will link the university and business in close alliance as partners in renewal.[4] "More than 85 percent of our graduates stay in the immediate area and keep banks, corporations, professional firms, and governmental institutions functioning," he points out, citing the importance of such

Cleveland State initiatives as the Advanced Manufacturing Center, which does applied research for many clients, including Ford Motor Company. Characterizing these academic-business partnerships as a blend of Adam Smith and John Henry Newman, Flower predicts that in the decades ahead such alliances will not be a luxury but a necessity.[5]

Examples of urban higher education's influence on the economy abound. In an article describing the ways in which higher education has been instrumental in helping to diversify North Carolina's economy, *The Chronicle of Higher Education* noted that the alliances between business and industry have been particularly visible in North Carolina's 58-campus community-college system, which has gained a high profile through its aggressive role in providing education in the workplace as well as literacy training for adults.[6] The state now has more than 700 sites where workplace education courses are offered, including many textile mills that are becoming automated and need knowledgeable employees to operate complex equipment.

The University of North Carolina at Charlotte (UNCC), located in the state's largest urban area, also has formed strong alliances with the corporate world, primarily through an adjacent research park that includes such tenants as Allstate, AT&T, IBM, Union Oil, and a number of computer firms. George Kuh and his coauthors describe the importance of UNCC's involvement with the community not only through the research park but also through University Place, a developing city that includes office and residential areas, a conference center, shopping facilities, recreational amenities, and green space.[7] UNCC also is one of five component campuses in North Carolina's Microelectronics Center, which is noted for basic research in semiconductors, computer-aided design, and integrated circuit design. The campus was founded as the Charlotte Center of the University of North Carolina at the end of World War II to serve the educational needs of returning veterans. Later, it became Charlotte Community College, added upper division courses in the early 1960s, and gained regional university status in 1965. With more than 13,000 students and a track record of impressive growth during the 1970s, UNCC is an outstanding example of the ways in which urban colleges and universities link with business and industry to drive the economy. For these institutions, success is not measured by a winning football team only, but rather by the results of their partnerships with the Fortune 500.

The knowledge pool is expected to double in the next 30 years, and as the late University of Houston president Marguerite Ross Barnett pointed out, "[I]f this were all theoretical knowledge without practical application, we would be faced only with a formidable information explosion."[8] But rapid changes in electronics, genetic research, and many other fields make it imperative that urban colleges and universities become partners in the development of these new research and knowledge-based companies. Through business-industry partnerships, urban campuses also provide assistance to emerging prototype firms. Barnett wrote: "Many university, business, civic, and political leaders realize that without some area for collaboration—whether a campus environment, research park, or technology center—regions may lose their margin of productivity. A changed economy will depend on the generation of new knowledge and systematic application of that knowledge through technology transfer."[9]

COMMUNITY PARTNERSHIPS

As far back as the 1920s, the late Parke Kolbe, who served as president of the University of Akron and later as president of Polytechnic Institute in Brooklyn, recognized the importance of linking the academy to the community. "The true urban university," he wrote, "must address itself to serving its urban environment."[10] While calling on urban universities to become more sensitive in their relations with neighboring residents, Old Dominion University professor Maurice Berube, author of a number of books on education and public policy, discusses the economic impact of these colleges and universities, not only in terms of the research they perform, which attracts subsidiary industries, but also as employers of area residents.[11] He cites Boston's colleges as the largest business in the city; the University of Pittsburgh as the second largest employer in that city; and Columbia as one of the most prosperous landowners in New York City.

Urban higher education's positive impact on America's cities is gaining wide recognition. In 1991 the Chicago Tribune article headlined "Colleges in America educate, invigorate" describes how 30 years ago the city of Toledo, Ohio, was brimming with vigor and prosperity, with large manufacturing firms thriving in the heart of the downtown business district.[12] The western half of the city did not have much to boast about. As the Tribune puts it, "There was lots of open space, a few subdivisions and a small, mediocre public college, a barely significant institution that catered to local kids who lacked the money or the grades to go to Ohio State." Today the picture is very different. Many of the large manufacturing corporations are gone, replaced by smaller firms and new businesses. The western half of Toledo is where the action is, due in large measure to the little college, which is not so little anymore. Now, the University of

Toledo, with approximately 25,000 students, is one of the fastest-growing schools in Ohio, pumping nearly $140 million into the local economy every year. The university is the center of Toledo's cultural life, with a new $10 million art school rising next to the city's highly regarded art museum. Its professors and laboratories serve as de facto research departments for some Toledo businesses, and over a recent four-year period the plastics industry funneled more than $2 million into the university's Polymer Institute, which is a vital part of the industry's research and development system.[13]

As the *Tribune* points out, not everyone is happy with the fact that urban colleges and universities are engaged in research for computer firms and polymer, electronics, pharmaceutical, and biochemical companies. Some raise questions as to whether such proprietary research will generate pressures on universities to shift their attention from basic scientific discovery toward applied research and product development. But as Toledo president Frank Horton noted, historically, most of the research in this country has not been publicly funded, and if higher education is to help the nation survive and compete in a global marketplace, both basic and applied research must be integral parts of the urban mission.

Like North Carolina, Ohio's urban colleges and universities are also actively engaged in initiatives that stimulate economic development. The Advanced Technology Center at Loraine County Community College, located in a heavily industrialized area outside of Cleveland and profiled in the 1988 book entitled *Higher Education in Partnership with Industry*, offers a prime example of urban higher education's efforts to maximize technology training in cooperation with the state.[14] The state invested $5.4 million in constructing and equipping the center and another $2 million in the purchase of equipment for advanced technology courses. Industry furnished additional equipment for the center, which boasts a state-of-the-art CAD/CAM system, computerized lathe and vertical mill, industrial robots, and training and electronic test equipment. A technology transfer resource center provides information to industrial clients as well as to faculty and students. The Loraine center offers education, training, and retraining in robotics, CAD/CAM, microelectronics, and process control, with formats and time schedules tailored to individual company needs. Additionally, the center is the home of the Ohio Technology Transfer Organization, which advises local businesses and industries on ways in which applying research, technological innovation, or training company personnel may help solve problems or contribute new knowledge to projects underway or being planned.

In an article describing a major university-business initiative, former University of Akron president William Muse tells how that institution linked with Case Western Reserve University in Cleveland and enlisted the region's polymer-related industries in a venture to capitalize on their combined technological leadership. The result was the Edison Polymer Innovation Corporation or EPIC. The venture was established with a $4.3 million state grant and 12 charter corporate partners based in northwestern Ohio. Today EPIC boasts approximately 70 corporate partners. Muse, who is now president of Auburn University, says:

> Despite the complexity and politics—linking two major universities, one public, one private, as well as private industry and the state of Ohio—EPIC is an excellent example of how universities can serve as a catalyst in sparking economic development. EPIC has attracted over $1 million in support so far from the likes of Monsanto, Shell, Goodyear, BF Goodrich, Dow and Dupont—companies that usually square off as fierce rivals. Their contributions have supported dozens of research projects at both universities, and a number of those are currently under consideration for commercial application.[15]

As vital as the connections between the enterprises of academe and commerce are, they are not without problems. Among the concerns that must be addressed are time and workload release for faculty, questions related to ethics and conflicts of interest, cultural differences between corporate managers and university researchers, publication and patent rights, contracts, and oversight procedures. Nevertheless, as University of California—Berkeley professors Stephen S. Cohen and John Zysman note, linkages between education, the industrial sector, and the service sector are critically important. Cohen and Zysman, both prolific writers in the areas of corporate strategy and the international economy, put it this way:

> Lose manufacturing and you will lose—not develop—those high-wage services. Nor is the relationship between high tech and manufacturing, like that between services and manufacturing, a simple case of evolutionary succession. If the United States wants to stay on top—or even high up—we can't just shift out of manufacturing into services. Nor can we establish a long-term preserve around traditional blue-collar jobs and outmoded plants. . . . In a world in which technology migrates rapidly and financial services are global, the skill of our workforce and the talents of our managers together will be our central resource.[16]

The information economy is said to be generating large numbers of new jobs that pay well. But the most challenging jobs—and the ones that pay the most—require workers with a high degree of competence coupled with the ability to analyze data and make sound judgments. In this fiercely competitive society, those who are undereducated will find themselves in unemployment lines or, worse yet, among the homeless who walk our cities' streets. Today, we hear a lot about safety nets—programs and institutions that ensure people are going to make it into the mainstream of American life. Unfortunately, many of those doors of opportunity are closing: the Armed Forces are taking fewer men and women; the labor union apprentice programs are shrinking; and secondary schools sometimes fail to equip young people for the competitive work force. Yet there is much evidence to suggest that urban campuses—with excellent academic programs, strong support services, and partnership links to the community—are the finest safety nets yet devised for our cities.

In an article about university-city partnerships in the South, the *New York Times* focused on the University of Alabama in Birmingham (UAB) as an example of the economic impact urban campuses have on the communities they serve.[17] The largest employer in Alabama, UAB operates the state's most comprehensive hospital, provides assistance to 90 public schools, performs research for a number of newly developing businesses, and has designed a model school in a new industrial research park. It is estimated that the economic impact on the region of UAB's hospital alone is about $1 billion a year. To strengthen the political bond between the university and the city, UAB granted leave to one of its faculty members to work on the staff of the city's first black mayor, Richard Arrington, Jr. The *Times* points out that just as land-grant colleges and universities were developed to bring public higher education to the country, with a mandate to focus on agriculture and mechanical arts, now urban universities have also changed the socioeconomic profile of people who are college-educated. In the past, only urban young people with solid family incomes were likely to leave home to attend college, but now urban campuses have brought higher education to the nation's population centers, making college a more convenient and affordable option for all. Of the Birmingham—UAB partnerships, the *Times* says:

> The story here has been repeated across the South, as urban universities have become the economic generators in their cities. As their economic importance has grown, these universities—in New Orleans, Charlotte, Atlanta and other cities—have also increased their

roles as community leaders, attacking social problems, preserving cultural institutions or generally filling a leadership role once played by business leaders. And they have played an equally important role in changing the character of the population around them, not only by providing employment but by making a college education more accessible to poor inner-city residents.[18]

Some state legislatures have begun to realize the increasingly important role urban colleges and universities play in sustaining cities. When its program funds were cut, Ohio's very successful urban higher education consortium convinced the legislature to reinstate $30 million in state financing by demonstrating the economic advantages the colleges bring to the state. Indeed, much of Ohio's success in university-community partnership linkages can be traced to the state's Urban University Program, which is patterned on the nation's land-grant model. Both this program and another—in interinstitutional urban research—were established in 1980 with funding by the Ohio legislature. The urban university initiative provides financial support to metropolitan university centers throughout the state to help them expand extension activities to Ohio's urban corridors in much the same way that the land-grant institutions worked through agricultural extension centers to bring assistance to the farmers. Based in the northeastern section of the state, the program ties together the urban and regional research, public service, and urban studies academic activities of the University of Akron, Cleveland State, Kent State, and Youngstown State.

Cleveland State's David Sweet, who chairs the Urban University Program, says lessons learned from failed urban extension experiments of the 1960s were incorporated into the design of the Ohio initiative, among them the principles of a committed client, one or more specified problems or issues, university advisers with genuine and relevant expertise, communication between the university adviser and the city client, and high quality, full-time staff.[19] Research efforts at Ohio's urban campuses have run the gamut from industrial retention problems to freight rates affecting trucking costs, real causes and potential solutions for homelessness, the economic impact of the savings and loan bailout on the recession, and Wright State's study of an economic development project in Montgomery County. The University of Akron helped the METRO Regional Transit Authority design a plan to boost its transportation market share, and the University of Cincinnati designed a computerized database of resources (federal, state, local, and private sector) available to fledging enterprises struggling for survival.[20]

The ways in which urban campuses form bonds with the community are quite diverse, ranging from structured programs such as Cleveland State's Urban Studies Center to less formal arrangements like UAB's sabbatical loan of a professor to the city's mayor. In the absence of substantive research, to judge one arrangement as "better" than another (for the university or the city) is subjective at best. The pathways to symbiotic and beneficial relationships are many. As with all partnerships, some university-business alliances will fail, and while further study is warranted on urban higher education's contributions to economic stability and development, there already exists a large body of favorable evidence.

In the state where I previously served, two major public universities, in a pioneering higher-education initiative, have developed over the past two decades the state's largest urban campus. Indiana University—Purdue University at Indianapolis (IUPUI), with 18 schools, 167 degree programs, and a student population that exceeds 27,000, plays a major role in the life of the state's capitol city. A few among its many business and community partnerships are these:

- The Near North Technology Transfer Center, a $6.5 million project designed to attract scientific and technological research to the city, is a partnership venture involving IUPUI, the city, state, and private industry. The center is the site of the Electronic Manufacturing Production Facility, a high-technology naval research center.
- The Indianapolis Center for Advanced Research, supported by IUPUI, the Chamber of Commerce, the Indianapolis Mayor's Office, and a private foundation known as the Showalter Trust.
- Project TEACH, a university-public school partnership aimed at helping alleviate the teacher shortage in urban schools.
- A major public-private health care initiative designed to help reduce the infant mortality rate in Indianapolis.

IUPUI chancellor Gerald Bepko says the location of his campus, within commuting distance of one-third of Indiana's population, gives it a crucial role in lifting the aspirations and advancing the knowledge and skills of area residents. Says Bepko, "Much of our nation's future will depend on the success of our cities, and much of our cities' vitality will come from the success of new models of higher education found increasingly at large urban campuses such as IUPUI."[21]

One of the most successful models of urban university-community interaction can be found in George Mason University, Fairfax, Virginia, which began in 1957 as a branch of the University of Virginia, with 17 students and a borrowed schoolroom. Now its student enrollment is in the 20,000 range and by the mid-1990s it is expected to surpass all other Virginia universities. Paula Odin, writer for *Virginia Business*, characterizes the university's School of Information Technology and Engineering (SITE) as GMU's first lesson in community interaction, describing how George Mason invited corporate leaders to join a university and industry alliance (the George Mason Institute) for an annual fee of $25,000.[22] Industry, it was reasoned, would benefit from faculty-planned research in high-technology areas. At first, no one was interested, so university leaders sat down with industry leaders to discover what *industry* would like. Soon, more than 40 area high-tech leaders had joined the institute. They went as a group to the state capitol, where they agreed to support the governor's proposed Center for Innovative Technology if he would support their graduate engineering school at GMU.

When the SITE proposal was submitted to Virginia's Council for Higher Education, the council said the new program might be all right, but GMU was not really talking about engineering. Odin quotes George Mason president Johnson as replying, "Like hell it isn't. If AT&T, TRW, and BDM say it's engineering, it's engineering!"[23] Now GMU has the country's only engineering school based on information technology with an enrollment that has passed the 2,200 mark, and industry has provided more than $2 million in support through scholarships, endowments, equipment and research contracts. Moreover, the George Mason Institute and its members have endowed eight professorships, and the School of Information Technology and Engineering has added a Center for Artificial Intelligence.

Just as higher education's linkages to cities are not limited to any one means of interaction—business, government, human services sector, or whatever—so, too, they are not limited to any one area of the country, or even to one type of institution. They are as far apart as Connecticut, Tennessee, and Florida and as varied in institutional mission as a public four-year university (Wichita State), state university urban campus (University of Tennessee at Chattanooga), and the nation's premier community college (Miami-Dade).

In Kansas, Wichita State is involved in a 13-member Sedgwick County economic development coalition that has formulated "Blueprint 2000," an $8.9 million plan for downtown Wichita revitalization, advanced technology transfer, improved transportation systems, a business and education compact, small business support systems, and a biomedical research institute.[24] Besides the university, other members of Sedgwick

County's "Partnership for Growth" include corporate leaders, city and county elected officials, and the Chamber of Commerce. Wichita State, which began as a Congregational liberal arts college in the nineteenth century, became a municipal university in the 1920s (as the University of Wichita), and gained its current title in 1964 as one of the Kansas Regents Institutions, is still very much identified as the "city's university." Among its far-reaching urban outreach initiatives are the innovative Center for Productivity Enhancement, a Center for Entrepreneurship, and the Institute for Aviation Research.

In Tennessee, a joint venture between the city and the University of Tennessee at Chattanooga resulted in a 12,000-seat arena being constructed with city funds on university land. The arena, which is used for entertainment purposes, also provides health and physical education facilities both for the university and the community. Marshall University president J. Wade Gilley, formerly Virginia's secretary of education, points to the significant community respect for UTC that is evidenced by the success of a regional campaign to endow nine chairs of excellence, representing programs of shared university community interest, with each chair underwritten by a $1 million endowment.[25] The university's research efforts have involved almost every aspect of city-county government and have provided a basis for reexamination of the metropolitan tax structure. Gilley cites UTC's "growing academic reputation that includes high ranking for the business school, a reputation of teaching excellence for the chemistry department, and recognition of the UTC Lupton Library, the first in the South to provide an on-line catalog system."[26]

In Florida, at Miami-Dade's thriving North Campus, officials have unveiled the first worldwide police vehicle simulator.[27] Touted as "the most sophisticated, state-of-the-art vehicle to train law enforcement drivers in an environment of a classroom that teaches real-life situations quickly and effectively," the simulator is available at M-DCC's School of Justice and Safety Administration. North Campus president J. Terrence Kelley said it was expected that the simulator would significantly reduce the cost of training police officers and, at the same time, save lives. An actual vehicle enhanced to transmit steering, shifting, acceleration, and braking commands to a system computer, the simulator was developed by M-DCC's School of Justice and Safety Administration, which was established in 1971 as a cooperative project involving the college and federal, state, county, and local governments. Five divisions of the school offer certification and licensing in various areas of law enforcement and public safety, including police training, private sector security training, fire department training, corrections training, and law enforcement assessment.

Miami-Dade, of course, offers a prime example of the very real contributions community colleges have made to urban America. With multiple campuses and the third largest enrollment (51,457 in 1991) of any college or university in the nation, M-DCC is involved in virtually every aspect of the huge metropolitan area it serves.[28] While community colleges, like their sister four-year institutions, have often wrestled with evolving definitions of their mission, there never has been any doubt about their commitment to the nation's cities, one that is well defined in a 1989 statement published by the American Association of Community and Junior Colleges:

> We view ourselves as catalysts and partners, beacons of opportunity and stability amidst our changing and challenging urban environment. We pledge, within the limits of our resources, to reach out to our neighborhoods, our schools, and our businesses to form partnerships for urban progress. . . . We reach out to all segments of our urban communities for partnerships as we strive together to deal with what may be the most significant issue of our time . . . the future of America's cities."[29]

That reaching out has taken many forms, from working to educate growing populations of new immigrants—which *Megratrends 2000* describes as "America's great import" and its key resource for competitive stature in a global economy—to training students for human services occupations and performing research for business and industry.[30] The scope of such community interaction is well illustrated at Seattle Central Community College, which is characterized by *Community College Week* as "an urban campus whose rainbow population mirrors America's impending majority of immigrants, women and people of color."[31] The SCCC campus is the home of one of the nation's four regional centers for the deaf and has one of the few interpretative learning programs on the West Coast. In recent years the city has been developing rapidly in the area of biotechnology, and in response to the industrial needs of Seattle, SCCC's faculty worked with industry leaders to develop a new two-year biotech program. The student mix at SCCC in 1991 was listed as 22 percent Asian, 11 percent African American, 5 percent Hispanic, and 2 percent Native American. Fifty-nine percent were women, and the countries represented in the campus population numbered 46.[32]

Virginia Commonwealth University president Eugene Trani and vice president and provost Charles Ruch have pointed out that urban campuses develop unique identities in large part because of the breadth and character of their interactions with their communities.[33] By design and conscious action, the authors assert, these institutions deliberately draw upon the rich tapestry and fabric of the community in strengthening their programs of instruction, research, and service. Trani and Ruch cite three characteristics that identify the nature of urban university-community interaction. First is the fact that it is mutually reinforcing, leaving both the institution and the environment richer for the participation. Second, the interaction is guided by institutional choice and strategy, and third, it is undergirded by value and import. In their words, "The university values and prizes the interactions, rewarding participants and building such interactions into the ongoing life of the institution. On the other hand, the community is reinforced and rewarded through its participation with the university. It welcomes and encourages university participation."[34]

One of the primary characteristics of the campus I previously served was an extensive involvement with health care, beginning with strong undergraduate programs in nursing, allied health sciences, dental auxiliary education, and pre-medicine, coupled with a very fine regional center of the university's School of Medicine. These strengths supported many community interactions, including my own involvement on the board of directors of a major hospital corporation; the university medical center's family practice partnership with another large hospital group; a university-community genetics clinic; research on industry's policies as they impact family wellness; studies of social service and health-care needs of the area's elderly; and faculty involvement with the Visiting Nurses Association, Hospice, and the State Board of Health. I mention these involvements because they are illustrative of one set of descriptors that derives from interactions beyond the boundaries of the campus. In part, these involvements derive from the nature of the metropolitan region that campus serves.

Another example of the way in which colleges and universities derive unique identities from their urban locations can be found in Valencia Community College, which is situated in the heart of a booming entertainment and film industry economy in Orlando, Florida, The *Urban Community Colleges Report* describes Orlando as a place where almost half the area's working population is employed by the tourist industry, where 2,500 new businesses are opened each month, where population swells by

102 people a day, and where the community college enrollment is surging at a rate of 10 percent per year.[35] In 1990–91 the college created 14 endowed chairs, including a $75,000 one in film making underwritten by Disney-MGM and other filmmakers.

Both Disney and Universal Studios have opened major production facilities in the Orlando area, creating a demand for various kinds of highly skilled technicians who can earn upwards of $20 an hour, with the most skilled earning up to $100,000 annually. To accommodate that demand, Valencia launched a new film program in 1988 using a $200,000 grant from the state of Florida to cover start-up costs. Matching funds were donated by Disney-MGM, including training equipment and studio use, and later Universal Studios contributed another $246,000. Two years after start-up, Valencia's Institute of Entertainment Technology awarded its first degrees in film production technology. By 1991 more than $1 million, including federal grants, had been contributed to the program, two productions had been produced by the Institute, and area residents had access to jobs in a new and thriving industry.[36]

The Orlando area also has experienced an enormous economic boost with the establishment of the University of Central Florida's vast research park, which now includes 70 companies employing some 4,000 employees. Peter Dagostino, chairman of the Economic Development Commission of Mid-Florida, has cited the Orlando International Airport, the University of Central Florida, and the UCF Research Park as cornerstones for economic development that will seek to take advantage of expanding opportunities in the global marketplace.[37] In an interview with *Central Florida Business*, Dagostino cited education as the key to retaining and recruiting industry, saying: "One thing that will make or break any economy is its school system. If we want to be a high-tech leader, we have to have a good education system."[38] Certainly, UCF with an outstanding College of Engineering, a doctoral program in human factors psychology, its Institute for Simulation and Training, and its Space Education and Research Center is a key component in the remarkable growth of metropolitan Orlando.

Through these kinds of commitments to and involvement with the extended community, urban colleges and universities have become a major intellectual, cultural, and economic resource for the nation as well as significant change agents for the society. Montreal mayor Jean Dore listed five advantages that these institutions provide large urban agglomerations:

- They permit the development of a work force that is skilled and able to adapt to change or, preferably, to initiate it.
- They allow local industry to benefit from the products of their research activity, and in turn they can take advantage of the expertise developed in the industrial sector.
- The presence of a skilled work force and the intensive technology transfer between universities and industry attract new enterprises. This creates a critical mass in certain sectors that can, therefore, become real centers of excellence for the city.
- In addition, academic institutions contribute to the international connections of their city, which further enhances the growth of commercial and cultural exchanges between the city and its partners.
- Finally, universities and other places of advanced knowledge contribute in a very striking fashion to a city's quality of life by providing people access to the cultural and intellectual riches the city produces.[39]

In the changing marketplace, urban colleges and universities are often spotlighted for their contributions to economic growth and preparation of the work force. But dollars-and-cents measures are woefully inadequate tools for quantifying the role of metropolitan campuses in the intellectual, cultural, and civic life of the community. Pick up any issue of the *Journal of Urban Affairs* or the *Urban Affairs Quarterly* and you will know how university research has touched every conceivable area of urban life, from studies of insurance redlining to public employee unions, land use, waste disposal, ground and air transportation, waterways, and port authorities. Pick up any issue of the daily newspaper and you will read of symphony concerts, theater productions, gallery exhibitions, poetry readings, dance performances, lectures, voter registration drives, health care and welfare forums, etc., sponsored by the local college or university, often in partnership with other community agencies. Virtually all are open to the public free or at very low cost.

In a chapter of their book forecasting a renaissance in the arts during the decade ahead, Naisbitt and Aburdene note that a "vibrant arts community is critical" when corporations decide where to locate and when people decide where to work.[40] They quote the director of MIT's Program on Neighborhood and Regional Changes as saying that 92 percent of Americans hold the view that arts are important to the quality of life in their communities. Where there are cities, there are universities. As Naisbitt and Aburdene say, "The affluent information society has laid the economic groundwork for the renaissance, creating new patrons whose wealth would make the Borgias green with envy. More important, it has spawned an educated, professional, and increasingly female work force . . . . Arts lovers tend to be educated; baby boomers are the most schooled generation in history."[41]

Urban campuses have always been at the heart of the cultural life of our cities, and today that role is stronger than ever. At the University of Missouri—Kansas City the campus serves as home to Missouri Repertory Theater. The 20-year-old repertory company has its own board, guarantees annual funding for the theater, and has raised an endowment for it. The theater employs an artistic director, UMKC employs the chairperson for the theater department, and together the artistic director and the department chairperson coordinate the academic and professional programs.[42] In Cape Girardeau, Missouri, the city linked up with Southeast Missouri State University to build a major regional civic center (the Show Me Center) on the campus. In Richmond, Virginia, the director of the Richmond Symphony holds an appointment at Virginia Commonwealth University.[43]

In Indianapolis, the university and the city have worked together in a number of positive ways involving construction and joint use of facilities, including the building of a new library, and the relocation of the university's Herron School of Art to a new downtown facility that serves as the home for music, dance, theater, and the visual arts. The University of Nevada—Las Vegas, named for two consecutive years by U.S. News and World Report as one of the "up and coming" universities in the nation, boasts a jazz ensemble that was named the 1990 National Champion and sponsors a broad range of musical and theatrical productions that draw community participation in the performing arts.

At George Mason University, 10 years of university-community collaboration led to the 1990 opening of a $30 million Center for the Arts, with major support coming from corporate and civic leaders. The center, with a concert hall that features a 75-foot tower, is a visual regional landmark and a focal point for the arts. Each year, women in the community stitch intricate masterpieces of embroidery, needlepoint, and appliqué, which are then auctioned off at a festive fund-raising gala to benefit the arts. During its first eight years, the university-community gala raised $1.5 million.[44]

PARTNERSHIPS WITH PUBLIC SCHOOLS

The links to city—the partnerships that strengthen economic, social, and cultural life—are crucial, but probably no area of university-community collaboration is more vital than is urban higher education's relationship to and involvement with the public schools. The demands facing the nation's elementary and secondary schools are no secret. They are as massive as they are pervasive, and they belong to us all. If the public schools fail, so do the colleges and universities. Education is a seamless pipeline, and a break at any point in that line—from kindergarten through university—means the whole of society is imperiled. Historically, outside of placing student teachers, few colleges and universities have formed strong alliances with the public schools in their communities, but in cities this has begun to change. Among urban colleges and universities is a growing realization that higher education has an enormous stake in the improvement of public schools. Not only are they the source of future students in higher education, they also are the wellspring of the work force and of leadership for the nation. As Frank Newman has pointed out, the greatest reform effort in the history of American education is happening right now, and it behooves urban campuses to become involved. "What needs to be done more broadly," says Newman, "is [for urban universities] to create coalitions of business and educators who understand their joint responsibilities to education at all levels."[45]

A number of efforts have been launched. The campus I previously served formed a partnership coalition with three urban public school districts, with support from the Lilly Endowment and the state of Indiana. The Urban Teacher Education Program, which received the 1990 Christa McAuliffe Award, is aimed at teacher education reform. University faculty and public schoolteachers work closely with university education majors, who spend more time in the "front lines" getting a feel for city school classrooms and learning how to relate to urban students. Characterized by *Education Week* as a "bold step away from the ivory tower," the program is exploring alternative certification processes, works closely with parents and community leaders in professional development centers, and has the backing of teacher unions and school administrators.[46]

The University of Louisville has undertaken more than 20 initiatives aimed at supporting Kentucky's Educational Reform Act of 1990, which mandates thousands of reforms for elementary and secondary education in that state.[47] The university's School of Education and its College of Arts and Sciences are assisting with the development of model programs to help the Louisville schools implement the new legislation's requirement of an "ungraded approach" through third grade to permit children to develop at their own pace without the pressures that traditional report cards bring. Additionally, the university's LATTICE Project on mathematics teaching and the Louisville Writing Project are being used as models for statewide learning programs.

Probably the most publicized urban university–public school partnerships have been forged in Boston, where in 1974, as part of a court-ordered desegregation settlement, the public schools were each paired with one or more of the local colleges and universities. Initially, the program was supported with state funds, but later philanthropic foundations and others provided support. The coupling of universities and public schools provided assistance to teachers and administrators, special instruction and tutoring for students, and involvement opportunities for parents. Altogether, 23 Boston-area colleges and universities participated in this pairing, forming the Boston Higher Education Partnership.

Ten years after its formation, a new formal agreement was signed between the Boston colleges and the schools calling for increased commitment by the colleges in helping college-bound students and in improving retention rates, both in the public schools and in the universities. By 1990 approximately $35 million had been invested by the participating Boston colleges in the form of scholarships for area high school graduates, nonstate funds raised for collaborative programs, and other direct aid.[48]

Community colleges also are forming an increasing number of public school alliances. Among those pioneering in these efforts is the Community College of Denver, which began with a program in the Cheltenham school in West Denver and quickly spread to 13 other sites throughout the city.[49] The Cheltenham project works with youngsters and their parents through an intergenerational literacy program which offers immigrant parents and their preschool children opportunities to improve their English skills. In Pittsburgh the community college has been working with three elementary schools through a cooperative arrangement with the school district. Its mission is to increase the potential for African American youngsters to move through the schools successfully and enter higher education.[50] Early intervention activities in math, reading, language, science, and social skills are provided in afternoon and weekend programs, with the project targeting students at the third grade and following them year by year until they are ready to enter college.

The success of urban campuses can best be gauged by their phenomenal growth and popularity, which is tied not simply to the quality of their academic programs and their location—though there can be no doubt that higher education must be delivered where "the action is" —but also to their interactive relationship with the metropolitan communities they serve. Success, both in the classroom and in the community, breeds success. Over the 10-year period from 1977 to 1987 enrollments at 32 urban college and universities studied by Portland State University researchers Kinnick and Ricks grew at twice the rate of their nonurban counterparts (12.9 percent compared to 6.5 percent).[51] In addition, among 89 colleges and universities listed in the 1993 *Chronicle of Higher Education Almanac* as having the largest enrollments, approximately one-third were urban institutions (see Figure 6.1).[52]

While they still are struggling with their own emerging identities, with public misconceptions of their role and mission, and such matters as budgetary constraints, urban campuses continue to move forward in positive and symbiotic relationships with America's cities. As the late Father Healy noted, the realities of trade and commerce impose themselves even on the life of the university, but they do not move in one direction only.

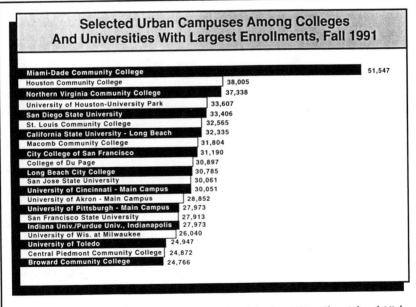

Selected Urban Campuses Among Colleges And Universities With Largest Enrollments, Fall 1991

Campus	Enrollment
Miami-Dade Community College	51,547
Houston Community College	38,005
Northern Virginia Community College	37,338
University of Houston-University Park	33,607
San Diego State University	33,406
St. Louis Community College	32,565
California State University - Long Beach	32,335
Macomb Community College	31,804
City College of San Francisco	31,190
College of Du Page	30,897
Long Beach City College	30,785
San Jose State University	30,061
University of Cincinnati - Main Campus	30,051
University of Akron - Main Campus	28,852
University of Pittsburgh - Main Campus	27,973
San Francisco State University	27,913
Indiana Univ./Purdue Univ., Indianapolis	27,973
University of Wis. at Milwaukee	26,040
University of Toledo	24,947
Central Piedmont Community College	24,872
Broward Community College	24,766

FIGURE 6.1   Among colleges and universities listed in the 1993 *Chronicle of Higher Education Almanac* as having the largest enrollments, about one-third were urban campuses.

Source: Figure drawn from information in *The Chronicle of Higher Education Almanac*, 25 August 1993, 12.

The city gives to the university its "deepest wells of talent . . . a rich mixture of colors, religions and origins."[53] The university gives back by serving the city's needs. At the 1985 Virginia Commonwealth University commencement, Father Healy described the role of the new urban campus this way:

> All universities use the same tools, the classic ones, but they are different in cities. . . . The humanities gather to themselves the new energies of new people, a welcome to diversity that renews the imagination and sends it haring to find beauties where they were least expected. All around you lies the stuff of social science, the vast mix of a major American city with its problems and its triumphs. . . . All [of the university's] skills, all its tools, are involved in quiet labor at the job Alfred North Whitehead outlined for universities; by making citizens, particularly new ones, you quietly remake the city itself.[54]

REFERENCES

1. Gary Orfield, "Public Policy and College Opportunity," *American Journal of Education* (August 1990): 325. First published by the University of Chicago 1990.
2. Ibid., 324.
3. John Naisbitt and Patricia Aburdene, *Megatrends 2000: Ten New Directions for the 1990s* (New York: Avon Books, 1990; reprint, New York: William Morrow, 1990), 17, 23, 25, 29, 33 (page citations are to Avon edition).
4. John A. Flower, "The Urban State University: Key to 21st Century America" (address to the National Press Club, Washington, DC, 4 April 1990).
5. Ibid.
6. *The Chronicle of Higher Education Almanac*, 28 August 1991, 80.
7. George D. Kuh et al., eds., *Involving Colleges* (San Francisco: Jossey-Bass, 1991), 247.
8. Marguerite Ross Barnett, "Urban Public Universities: The Promise and the Peril," *Higher Education & National Affairs* (4 July 1988), 7.
9. Ibid.
10. Parke Kolbe, *Urban Influences in Higher Education in England and the United States* (New York: Macmillan, 1928), quoted in Maurice Berube, *The Urban University in America* (Westport, CT: Greenwood Press, 1978), 12–13.
11. Berube, *The Urban University in America*, 11.

12. Jon Margolis, "Colleges in America Educate, Invigorate," *Chicago Tribune*, 5 May 1991, sec. 1, pp. 21, 27.
13. Ibid.
14. David R. Powers et al., eds., *Higher Education in Partnership with Industry* (San Francisco: Jossey-Bass, 1988), 48–49.
15. William Muse, "A Catalyst for Economic Development," *Metropolitan Universities* 1 (Spring 1990): 84.
16. S. S. Cohen and J. Zysman, "The Myth of Post-Industrial Economy, *Technology Review* (February–March 1987): 54–62.
17. Karen De Witt, "Universities Become Full Partners to Cities in South," *New York Times*, 13 August 1991, A-12.
18. Ibid.
19. David C. Sweet, "Working for Ohio's Future: The First Decade" (a report on the Ohio Urban University Program, 1991).
20. Ibid.
21. "Indiana University—Purdue University at Indianapolis by the Year 2000: Extending the Promise 1991–1993" (campus marketing recruitment publication, IUPUI, Indianapolis, 1991), 16.
22. Paula Odin, "GMU's Gospel of Interaction," *Virginia Business* (August 1989), 15–17, 19–22.
23. Ibid., 19.
24. "Economic Partnership/Wichita Sedgwick County, Kansas," *Metropolitan Universities* 1 (Spring 1990): 105.
25. J. Wade Gilley, *The Interactive University: A Source of American Revitalization* (Washington, DC: The American Association of State Colleges and Universities, 1990), 40–41, 62.
26. "Miami-Dade Unveils First Worldwide Police Vehicle Simulator," *Community College Week*, 23 December 1991, 2.
27. *The Chronicle of Higher Education Almanac*, 28 August 1991, 12.
28. Maurice D. Weidenthal, "Who Cares about the Inner City? The Community College Response to Urban America," (Washington, DC: Association of Community and Junior Colleges, 1989), 1.
29. Ibid.
30. Naisbitt and Aburdene, *Megatrends 2000*, 25.
31. "Dr. Charles H. Mitchell: From the Gridiron to the Presidency," *Community College Week*, 2 September 1991, 15.
32. Ibid.
33. Charles P. Ruch and Eugene P. Trani, "Scope and Limitations of Community Interactions," *Metropolitan Universities* 1 (Fall/Winter 1991): 27.
34. Ibid., 28.
35. Maurice D. Weidenthal, ed., "Working Magic in Orlando's Booming Kingdom," *Urban Community Colleges Report* 2 (June 1991): 1.

36. Maurice D. Weidenthal, "Hollywood East Goes to College," *Urban Community Colleges Report* 2 (June 1991): 2.
37. Dick Marlowe, "Competing for Cleanest Industries," *Central Florida Business*, 25 November–1 December 1991, 3.
38. Ibid.
39. Jean Dore, "A City and Its Universities: A Mayor's Perspective," *Metropolitan Universities* 1 (Spring 1990): 29–30.
40. Naisbitt and Aburdene, *Megatrends 2000*, 63.
41. Ibid.
42. Ruch and Trani, "Scope and Limitations of Community Interactions," 31.
43. Ibid.
44. Paula Odin, "A Focal Point for the Arts," *Virginia Business* (August 1989): 21.
45. Frank Newman, "Anatomy of the Urban University," *Metropolitan Universities* 1 (Fall–Winter 1990–91): 98.
46. Blake Rodman, "A Bold Step from the Ivory Tower: Three Midwestern Cities Are Cooperating to Train Their Own Teachers on the Job," *Education Week* 7, no. 39 (22 June 1988): 21, 23.
47. *University of Louisville, 1990–91 Annual Report*, 18–19.
48. Daniel H. Perlman, "Diverse Communities, Diverse Involvements," *Metropolitan Universities* 1 (Spring 1990): 96.
49. Maurice D. Weidenthal, "Can We Make a Difference in Elementary Schools?" *Urban Community Colleges Report* 2 (May 1991): 2.
50. Ibid.
51. Mary K. Kinnick and Mary F. Ricks, "The Urban Public University in the United States: An Analysis of Change, 1977–1987" (paper presented at the Twenty-Ninth Annual Forum of the Association for Institutional Research, Baltimore, MD, 30 April–3 May 1989).
52. *The Chronicle of Higher Education Almanac*, 28 August 1991, 12.
53. Timothy Healy, commencement address, Virginia Commonwealth University, Richmond, VA, 18 May 1985.
54. Ibid.

CHAPTER
seven
· · · · · · · ·

Urban Promise: Preparing for the Twenty-first Century

Author Kurt Vonnegut, following a 1991 lecture at the 27,000-student Indiana University—Purdue University campus in Indianapolis, wrote the following letter to Chancellor Gerald Bepko, addressing it in care of Stardust University, 355 North Lansing Street, Indianapolis, Indiana 46202–2896:

> Dear Chancellor Bepko—
>
> I am unsurprised by the grace and wit and letterhead of your letter of five days ago. I lecture at all sorts of colleges and universities, and find torpor in the schools social climbers send their kids to, and all sorts of merriment and hope in urban schools like yours, whose diplomas are not famous for being tickets to establishments of the ruling class. Your students are miles ahead of the Ivy League, since they feel no obligation to pretend that America is something it obviously isn't. I believe as you do that, fifty years from now or less, all over the world people are going to be asking where all these wonderful, realistic, honorable leaders came from, and . . .
>
> Cheers,
> Kurt Vonnegut

This ringing endorsement is music to the ears of many urban educators, who hope, and believe, that such a prediction about future leadership is a prophetic indication of the accomplishments for which urban campuses will one day be recognized. Mr. Vonnegut's praise and encouragement notwithstanding, however, the eventual achievements of urban higher education will be determined, in part, by external factors over which they may have little control. Clearly, for a group of energetic institutions which as yet cannot agree even on a name or definition for themselves, the future is far from certain.

While enumerating probabilities and discussing promise are safer and certainly more appropriate at this early stage of urban campus evolvement, some generalizations about urban colleges and universities can be made even now. At the outset, one point should be made quite clear: No one could or should argue that urban campuses will replace all or any of the existing models of higher education now recognized and tucked safely into established taxonomies. This point is extremely important because the failure to understand it has resulted in needless territorial concerns on the part of many nonurban campuses, not to mention a long laundry list of frustrations for urban institutions. These frustrations, fueled by misunderstandings and competitive efforts, are major millstones weighing heavily on their progress. Such impediments in higher education must be removed if all colleges and universities are to fulfill their role in the twenty-first century.

Certainly, over time all of the known models in higher education will change in multiple ways—relative size, impact, available resources, academic programs, to name a few. In a very real sense, the diversity of the American system of higher education has provided a "customized" approach. Public schools, private schools, religious schools, single-sex schools, colleges and universities that emphasize programs from teacher education to marine biology all exist in the nation. We have land-grant universities, sea-grant universities, and, with the authorization of Title XI of the Higher Education Act, we have urban-grant universities.

I do not suggest that any one institutional model is unimportant for its constituency, for a variety of reasons, one constituency—the more than three-quarters of American citizens who live in metropolitan areas—has grown enormously and is continuing to grow. The emerging urban model which serves that constituency deserves the same sensible consideration of its issues and needs—as well as the same respect for its contributions—as has been accorded others in higher education. The likelihood that any of the known types of colleges and universities which now exist will vanish from higher education's landscape is remote. Certainly, urban campuses are not in the business of trying to put others *out* of business. What they are engaged in, and what they energetically pursue, is the development of programs and support services that will effectively provide quality education for their students as well as the support required to allow the significant research opportunities for their faculties to be undertaken and realized. In a time of economic expansion this task might not be so difficult as it is in these days of frugality and restriction. In better times, needs could be served by increases in funding from local, state, federal, private, or tuition dollars. In a flat economy, however, additional dollars for support of urban institutional growth often must be realized in competitive ways. It is in this competitive environment that urban institutions are unfairly disadvantaged. Liberal arts colleges and research universities are known entities whose purpose and importance are well recognized. Urban colleges and universities often are not so well understood.

The short-term outcome of competition for resources will likely continue to accrue to the advantage of older, more familiar kinds of higher education institutions, if for no other reason than that present-day legislators and donors know and understand such institutional models. Additionally, established campuses with longer histories usually have greater numbers of well-placed alumni and friends who stand ready to support them and to lobby on their behalf. Most well-endowed higher education institutions—public and private alike—also have significant resource bases and can afford more professional staff to assist in the ongoing search for funding, particularly in the research arena. Finally, when grants and awards require matching dollars, urban campuses, with a smaller resource base, are again less likely to win those awards.

Former University of Hartford president Stephen Joel Trachtenberg has written about the competition for resources and predicts increasing stratification in higher education.[1] He envisions institutions such as Harvard, Swarthmore, Chicago, and Stanford becoming preserves "for the rich and the smart" while taxpayer-supported colleges and universities struggle to deliver higher education in decaying facilities, to excessively large classes, and with outmoded equipment. He also predicts that access to higher education will become increasingly restricted, at the same time pointing out that technology "*could* be used to distribute wealth more widely to a relatively leisure population, or it *could* be used solely to fulfill the needs of an upper class—leaving the under class permanently unemployed." Trachtenberg, now at George Washington University, adds these words of caution:

> There is no intrinsic reason why newly stratified schools cannot serve the needs of an equally stratified economy. Even today we can see how the children of the upper middle class are steered into elementary and high school systems that steadily widen their advantage over those youths who remain in school systems in decaying inner cities

and industrial areas. To the extent that marketplace considerations alone determine the shape taken by institutions of higher education—to the extent, above all, that scholarship aid and loans are no longer made available at the federal or state level—to that extent we will educationally disenfranchise a large and probably growing portion of the U.S. population.[2]

The circumstances Trachtenberg outlines are not inconceivable. To the extent that urban colleges and universities continue to be perceived as a threat to existing models rather than as an effective and necessary resource for educating the growing majority of the population, to that extent his pessimism may be warranted. In that light, the urgency of clarifying the importance of urban institutions becomes quite apparent.

MEETING NEW EDUCATIONAL DEMANDS

Sadly, even in academe there are those who have strong biases against support for urban colleges and universities because the belief is that these institutions very often do not enforce rigid and highly selective admissions policies. Some even go so far as to argue that substantive investments should be made *only* in the campuses with the brightest students. Institutions providing access to students who have been less well prepared and to those who have been historically underserved are not deemed worthy of significant resources. Of course, such an argument was never logical or well founded. The increasing numbers of doctoral and medical degree-holders who earned their first degrees at urban campuses provide solid evidence that the claim is void of credibility.

As large numbers of older students knock at the doors of urban higher education, flexible admissions standards must be employed if they are to be educated for the competitive society in which they live and raise their families. As Indiana University professor Louis Holtzclaw has pointed out, even adult students with very poor previous postsecondary records can do exceptionally well.[3] Holtzclaw reports that in a research survey of general-studies degree students admitted provisionally during the period from 1977 to 1985, those who took courses did very well overall, recording a B to B-minus average, which was almost as high as regularly admitted students. As an example, he cites a student who at age 30 was functioning as an aerospace engineer with a major corporation in spite of the fact that he had neither a high school diploma nor a GED. Admitted provisionally, after traditional admissions requirements were waived, he immediately began to make straight A's in three courses.[4] As one urban educator has noted, urban colleges and universities should be judged on "who they let out" not on "who they let in," which is the true indicator of the quality of the institution. Nevertheless, admissions practices sometimes continue to be used in ways that mitigate against urban institutions in the competition for resources.

The fact that urban campuses enroll relatively higher percentages of minority students is a source of great pride to urban educators, who are at the same time painfully aware that some educators, both inside and outside the academy, characterize minority students in somewhat negative terms—as ill-prepared, poor achievers, unmotivated, or unlikely to succeed. Such racial biases serve only as barriers against the goal of a prosperous and peaceful society. Faith Paul's 1991 report on a study that examined educational opportunity structures, access, and bachelor's degree attainment for metropolitan undergraduate students attending colleges in Chicago, Houston, Los Angeles, and Philadelphia between 1975 and 1986, revealed that opportunities available through the public colleges and universities have been most important for all groups of students.[5] Paul writes:

> The findings from this research showing the strong progress of white students across the metropolitan areas and the serious losses for Hispanic and black students in access, opportunity, and success at all types of colleges and universities and at all levels of selectivity are very important. They point to very different experiences for inner-city and outer-rim students in the large metropolitan areas of this country and raise important questions about whether such differences can and should be tolerated.[6]

Paul also notes that important strides in access for minorities, made during the 1960s and 1970s, dwindled during the early 1980s as attitudes, policies, and economic and social conditions changed. "The moral conscience of the nation has not been reawakened," Paul adds, "but its economic conscience is stirring, and concerns about the loss of potential human resources at a time of scarcity may impel action."[7] Since recent figures indicate new progress is being made in minority enrollment and graduation rates, perhaps Paul's observations about the nation's stirring economic conscience are coming to pass. Considering the economic and social consequences to urban campuses caused by racial bias, one can only hope it will rapidly die a well deserved death.

To fail to develop and support urban institutions fully for very much longer would be to fail to support the educational needs of the majority of the population seeking higher education (see Figures 7.1 and 7.2). Equally important, it would be particularly detrimental to minorities and to economically disadvantaged members of society who reside, for the most part, in urban centers. The results of limiting urban campus development could very well become a vicious cycle in which underserved populations most in need of access to higher education continue to be thwarted in their goals. Blocking access to those who possess both the will and the ability to contribute at high levels would serve not only to depress the economy but to heighten social unrest.

In 1991 Kim Huggett of the Chabot-Las Positas Community College District in California noted that the community college system in that state would lose an estimated $225 million to $270 million in 1991–92 and that in the previous fiscal year alone some 8,000 students were served without support.[8] He also pointed out that 83 percent of the minority students in California's higher education system are enrolled in community colleges, where a system-wide population increase of 30 to 50 percent is projected over the next 15 years. Judith Eaton, director of the American Council on Education's National Center for Academic Achievement and

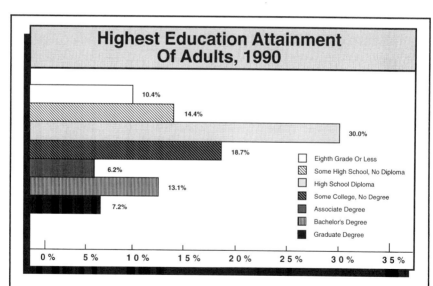

FIGURE 7.1   U.S. Census Bureau statistics for 1990 reveal that only 13.1 percent of adults 25 and older hold bachelor's degrees, and less than one-third have earned high school diplomas. As the knowledge explosion continues, however, the best jobs will go to those with the highest levels of education and skills.

Source: Figure drawn from information in *The Chronicle of Higher Education Almanac*, 25 August 1993, 14; based on U.S. Census Bureau statistics covering adults aged 25 and older.

Transfer, has noted that many urban colleges provide the key point of access for many low-income and minority students and has insisted that investment in community colleges must be much greater. Said Eaton, former president of the Community College of Philadelphia, "I, as well as several other community college leaders, have been arguing that for years."[9]

Even though the number of U.S. citizens living in poverty is slowly declining, cities are still home to a substantial number of those who are economically disadvantaged. John Kasarda, director of the Kenan Institute of Private Enterprise at the University of North Carolina, outlined the problem in an article in Newsweek magazine, noting that as cities have shifted away from manufacturing and goods processing, blue-collar jobs have virtually been eliminated.[10] As the service sector has replaced manufacturing, new jobs in the city require employees who are skilled in reading and math. Kasarda warns that the changing demographics of the cities "are on a collision course" with the rising skill requirements of the urban job market.[11] Clearly, resources have to shift and priorities must be rethought, if urban campuses are to serve this growing constituency in an effective way.

Despite all of the impediments detailed in this chapter, resources must and *will* become available to institutions serving the New Majority. Progress in this regard cannot be denied. Whether campus growth comes from "suburban-collar" communities, from the inner city, or from both is immaterial. The whole can be no stronger than the sum of its parts, and all "parts" of the metroplex, from core cities to urban beltways to outer-rim suburbs, have educational needs that must be met.

The U.S. Department of Education estimates that the number of college students will climb from 14.1 million in 1991 to 16 million in 2002, with a greater growth in minority enrollments, the number of female students rising at twice the rate of male students, and with a growing proportion of students expected in the age-group 35 and older.[12] Commenting on the projections in an article carried by the *Chronicle of Higher Education*, Elaine El-Khawas, vice-president for policy analysis and research at the American Council on Education, said, "In our society, beginning workers need some college-level training. Jobs for high school graduates have dried up, and college training has become the new minimum."[13]

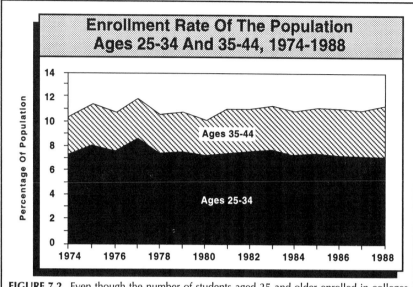

FIGURE 7.2   Even though the number of students aged 25 and older enrolled in colleges and universities rose by nearly 2 million between 1974 and 1988, the percentage of the population enrolled in higher education has varied only slightly over the years.

Source: Cecilia A. Ottinger, ed., *Higher Education Today: Facts in Brief,* American Council on Education, 1992, 65; based on U.S. Department of Commerce, Bureau of the Census, Current Population Reports. *School Enrollment,* Series P-20, as summarized in *Enrollment by Age: Distinguishing the Numbers from the Rates,* ACE's Research Brief Series, Vol. 1, No. 7, 1990.

PREPARING STUDENTS FOR A CHANGING SOCIETY

As I have stressed throughout this book, as the knowledge explosion continues and the rate of change accelerates, people nationwide also will need advanced education throughout their life-span. They are not going to be able to sell their homes and move every time they need new and more knowledge. Urban colleges and universities are only just beginning to witness the enormous impact of the demand for continuing reeducation. As old businesses, professions, and industries die, people will need to learn new jobs and skills. While upgrading knowledge has been common-place in law and medicine, now reeducation will take place at beginning and intermediate levels as well. Community college programs and undergraduate certificates will be in as much, or perhaps even greater, demand than postbaccalaureate updating. In the coming decade, the number of associate degrees awarded is expected to rise by 15 percent; bachelor's degrees are likely to increase by 12 percent; and doctoral degrees are predicted to increase by 7 percent.[14]

Realistically, continuing redevelopment of the population, if it is to be successful in meeting societal needs, must exhibit two characteristics that were highlighted on an American Association of State Colleges and Universities poster proclaiming, "close to perfect, close to home." The demand is real, for today's citizens are learning that the dynamics of our time require that they must have ready access to high-quality education. The majority of these citizens are not attorneys, physicians, or high-level corporate managers who can afford to take time away from their work or who can afford to pay large sums for travel in order to update themselves through seminars in Aspen, Palm Springs, or Honolulu. Such executive models have served well the intellectual renewal needs of affluent professionals, but relatively few are able to participate in them. Increasingly, a broader body of people will be needing reeducation. For many of them, reeducation will be just that—a time for renewal through learning, a time for finding and training in a brand new field.

Jerome Ziegler explores the role of urban colleges and universities in preparing citizens for the changing nature of both work and the family in the twenty-first century society.[15] Ziegler says he considers the two issues in a singular context "because the nature of family structure today is greatly influenced by the economy." He explains it this way:

> The change from an economy based on the manufacturing and extractive industries to one of services and information has been massive and sudden. Our society has not yet caught up with it. Although some of its effects are clear, such as the effect on male breadwinners, this transition is not well understood. We are only beginning to fathom what new educational and social policies and programs the country needs in order to train the workforce for the next century, and how work and the lack thereof affects family structure.[16]

To continue to relegate urban colleges and universities to a lower rung on the ladder of funding and to assign them a low priority in approval processes for academic programs would be more than foolhardy; it would also amount to social and economic suicide for, as Ziegler points out, "it is the city, writ large, that remains the dominant influence in our society."[17]

GAINING SUPPORT

Even with continuing misperceptions about the nature of their students, the quality of their research, and their place in the higher education taxonomy, urban campuses can expect that their prospects for support will increase over time. If not accomplished by sound public policy, it will be accomplished in other ways. One fact above all others stands them in good favor: In the not too distant future, urban campuses will have educated a significant share of the nation's college and university graduates—and the pool of urban alumni will continue to expand. As this occurs, one can reasonably predict that increasingly larger numbers of urban-educated workers will hold key positions in virtually all fields, including policy making. For them, freshman beanies, halls of ivy, fraternity parties, and other time-honored traditions of the older, once familiar campus models will be replaced by the affectionate memories of a close-to-home campus that offered them a supportive environment, an excellent academic program, and, quite often, an opportunity to work their way through college while also providing for their families. These campuses are moving rapidly toward the time when they will be as well understood and as familiar to city, state, and national leaders as are traditional campuses to most of the leaders of today. Moreover, urban campuses also will serve as the continuing lifeline to economic viability for their communities.

COMMUNITY ASSETS

Many urban campuses already have moved well beyond their walls into urban-grant activities similar to those of their land-grant colleagues, and as a result they have begun to experience the support of major political power structures in the cities they serve. While cities in the past often viewed the local college campus primarily as a necessary nuisance, today most cities tout their colleges and universities as the major driving force of communal progress. Cities have discovered the worth of higher education, and what is valued generally receives support and protection.

The *New York Times*, in an August 1991 article about urban campuses in the South, notes that as the profile of urban institutions has risen so has their ability to attract "star talent" and major financial support.[18] The *Times* recounts how, after persuading the Coca-Cola Company to endow a jazz chair at its institution, the University of New Orleans got Ellis Marsalis, a highly regarded teacher and the father of jazz musicians Wynton and Branford Marsalis, to be the first musician to hold that chair.

The university then helped revive the New Orleans Symphony in what the *Times* describes as "a typical example of the community-university links that have developed." These kinds of examples will only grow in number as urban campuses expand and form stronger bonds with the communities they serve.

Central to the strengthening of these bonds is the research support that well-trained "local" scholars produce and bring to bear on difficult urban issues. Indeed, the potential of urban faculty for excellence in research outcomes cannot be minimized. Moreover, the opportunity to share state-of-the-art equipment owned by nearby businesses and agencies is a singular advantage for urban faculty in a time when the cost of instrumentation is limiting activity even for well-endowed research universities. Although they are significantly less dependent on equipment, faculty in the social sciences and professional schools also are ideally positioned because of the ready availability of the enormous data bases large population centers provide. The arts and humanities also experience major advantages in the urban setting, where additional galleries, libraries, and museums provide extensions of those available on any campus.

With the funding in 1991 of the Urban Grant University Program, colleges and universities in metro America face even greater opportunities to participate in joint ventures for economic development, school reform, public works improvements, and arts enhancement. The new grant program is totally unlike the old Ford Foundation urban laboratory of the 1960s, which was unsuccessful because cities and campuses collided as they failed to define and work toward mutually beneficial goals. Today's grants require that collective goals be worked out as the proposals are developed, with special consideration going to those coalitions that have already experienced successful collaboration. The program, originally authorized, but not funded, by Congress in 1980, now provides federal financing for the kinds of city-university partnerships that have flourished around the country for more than a decade. In supporting passage of the grant program, which is part of the Higher Education Act, U.S. Representative Thomas Sawyer of Ohio, a cosponsor along with Oregon's Senator Mark Hatfield, said, "Urban universities form a very special function in education. That same engine that drove the economy of this nation during the shift from agriculture to urban industrial dominance has the same potential in an urban setting."[19]

As student populations and resources of the urban-grant institutions grow, they will be able to provide even greater assistance to the nation's cities through their laboratories, classrooms, shared technology, and faculty expertise. In the same way that agricultural and engineering schools transferred knowledge that had a major impact on the society during the last 100 years, the synergistic links between campuses and cities today will accrue to the benefit of both in the century to come. The University of Central Florida, George Mason University, and Miami-Dade Community College are just a few of the institutions that demonstrate this special kind of synergism as they work with the tools of the academy in partnership initiatives that benefit the regions they serve. As Lynton and Elman point out:

> Here and abroad, "technology transfer" has become a new motto. To date, the term has often been narrowly interpreted to mean university-industry cooperation in research and development. But there exists growing recognition that scientific and technological innovations are tools, useful only to the extent to which they are absorbed and used in traditional portions of the economy. . . . This more pervasive kind of technology transfer requires the mutually interdependent combination of research, instruction, and extension that characterized the traditional land-grant college. If the potential of modern technology is to be fully realized, there is little doubt that the basic idea of extension should be resurrected.[20]

In recent years, report after report has emphasized the need for higher education to take a lead in turning the economy and the society around. *To Secure the Blessings of Liberty*, a report of the National Commission on the Role and Future of State Colleges and Universities, called for the expansion of human capital through education and training, generating new technologies, new products, and new services through basic and applied research and by helping businesses maintain their competitive edge.[21] Bell pointed out that higher education for the masses will become critical as educational requirements for the knowledge society become more stringent. Two other major publications, *Time for Results: The Governors' 1991 Report on Education* (the National Governors' Association) and *Transforming the State Role in Undergraduate Education* (the Education Commission of the States), called upon higher education to become more involved in economic development and in preparing the nation's work force for the demands of a globally competitive marketplace.

In the 1980s, higher education's renewal initiatives focused on the curriculum—what should constitute an undergraduate course of study, how learning should be assessed, and so forth. In the decade ahead, efforts will need to emphasize ways the academy must change in order to serve the new and growing needs of the society. Problems related to race, class, and economics must be addressed within the framework of educational priorities. With only three million students—about 20 percent of the total college population—enrolled full-time, in residence, and younger than 22 years of age, urban institutions must emerge as leaders in the delivery of higher education to adults.[22] The College Board estimates that approximately 80 million adults are now in their primary learning years, ages 35 to 44. Most of them live in cities.

The challenges are great. Talk that the "open door" to higher education is closing must cease. If anything, the door will have to open wider. With assistance, urban population centers and urban campuses can accomplish the task, but the entire higher education community will need to be supportive. It is as pointless to pretend that urban campuses are somehow illegitimate offspring of established institutions as it is foolish to perceive them as a threat. Reality and necessity require that they be recognized and respected as peers, that they be given a legitimate place in the taxonomy, and that they be brought into the "fold." When these goals are accomplished, all of higher education will be enriched, for only a robust economy can generate the kind of resources that all of academe requires. As the 1991 Governors' Report warned, "access without quality is a cruel deception, while quality without access is a betrayal of the cherished American ideal of equal opportunity."[23] To Secure the Blessings of Liberty put it another way: "[W]ithout quality in education, the nation loses its strength. Without equity in education, democracy ceases to function."[24]

One final observation also can be made about urban campuses. While it is too soon to say exactly how they will be defined, the fact that they are not carbon copies of the traditional campuses is in large part the result of their serving students whose needs are different from traditional students. There are exceptions, of course. Among the more notable ones is Columbia College in Chicago, a distinguished and extraordinary private institution. On the public side is Cleveland State University, which was chartered as Ohio's urban university.

Ernest Spaights, Harold Dixon, and Susan Nickolai discuss the distinctive nature of emerging institutions in this way:

> Urban universities are specialized institutions as surely as the Massachusetts Institute of Technology is specialized. In order to be specialized, however, the urban university must recognize its urban mission,

fulfill its obligation to the city in which it lies, and permeate its institutions with an academic zeal for urbanness. . . . As we approach the twenty-first century, the population of metropolitan areas continues to grow. With this growth in population comes the attendant problems of people living in close proximity to each other. Consequently, the urban university truly dedicated in its mission to urban areas and interested in improving the quality of life for urban residents can have a powerful, lasting impact on millions of lives.[25]

TRENDS IN URBAN HIGHER EDUCATION

By in large, however, most urban institutions have not fully defined themselves and are still moving toward what they will eventually become. As George Mason's vice president J. Wade Gilley has pointed out, "The early twentieth-century notions of outpost extension centers and branch campuses are wholly inappropriate solutions for the emerging post-industrial regions of the twenty-first century, which require the ambience of a major university to achieve full potential."[26] It seems to me that urban campuses are traveling along at least four trend lines, with most institutions exhibiting one or more aspects of all four.

The first of these trends is something like the "normal school" that developed as a means of preparing professional teachers. In most cases, the normal school evolved into a teachers' college and later into a comprehensive university. In the normal school phase, however, the prime emphasis was professional education. Other academic courses were valued, but generally in the sense that they were perceived as secondary areas of learning, necessary only in support of or as auxiliary to the professional component. Normal schools were quite good at what they did and succeeded in turning out a great many well-trained teachers for the nation's schools. Some urban campuses exhibit striking similarities to this early model, which has as its overriding goal the production of students who are professionally credentialed. All other academic pursuits are valued only as they relate to the ultimate end of professional accreditation. It is in no way surprising that this model should be a popular one since many urban students are first-generation college-goers who see higher education in a very narrow sense—as a means of preparing for the world of work. In this conceptual framework, learning is valued only in its relationship to job preparation. While the professional or normal school model has much to recommend it, and while career goals certainly are reasonable expectations for students, clearly urban institutions need to make a concerted effort to broaden students' perspectives so that they reach beyond vocational assumptions about the process and outcomes of a college education.

A second trend of urban campuses involves the tendency to clone another institutional model. The inclination to follow the lead of traditional colleges and universities is quite natural, of course, since most decision makers in urban higher education were educated in those kinds of settings. The assumption here is akin to the notion that it is not necessary to reinvent the wheel. After all, if it worked well for me when I attended the university, it should work well for students who are pursuing their degrees today. Sometimes, however, doing things as they have always been done leads to obvious absurdities. Among these (and one over which few campuses have any control) is the continuation of the traditional academic calendar. New Majority students are perpetually frustrated at being forced each summer to slow their educational progress. This situation exists because campus funding and faculty appointments are predicated on the traditional two-semester calendar, with only abbreviated sessions between May and September. Logical thinking would lead one to the realization that New Majority learners will not be going home to "get in the crops," "find a summer job," or simply to "grow up." Nevertheless, because this was the way it was done in another time and in other places, students and universities often must wait out the summer for reasons that are not remotely applicable to their lives in a contemporary urban setting.

The trend to cloning of traditional models has other inherent flaws as well. Even the language of another institutional model is troublesome. I once enthusiastically engaged in an effort to introduce students more effectively to the intellectual rigors of college by providing them a special class that was quite seriously referred to as the Freshman Seminars. Those of us who planned the seminars, however, failed to take into account that a New Majority student could very well be a freshman for several years. In retrospect, we realized that an introduction to college in a student's fifth semester wouldn't make much sense.

A third trend exhibited by urban campuses is built around the land-grant model and incorporates extensive applied research initiatives and major outreach activities. Indeed, almost all urban colleges and universities exhibit characteristics of the land-grant institution. As far back as 1978 Maurice Berube suggested that while the "agrarian myth" had promoted a national hostility to the city and had adversely influenced the development of urban campuses, the land-grant university model, if appropriately adapted, could very effectively serve the cities.[27] Berube went so far as to propose a federal college system that would be comprised of highly autonomous colleges in cities throughout the country.[28] He was correct about the research and service opportunities for urban campuses. Political scientists find themselves dealing with issues of election reform; colleges of education find themselves involved in school reform; medical schools operate community health-care clinics, and the list goes on. Still, while there is a natural proclivity toward the land-grant model, the complexities of the urban environment require the development of a model more specifically designed for the time. The problems of the city are sometimes more varied and complex than those faced by land-grant institutions in an agro-industrial age.

Finally, for lack of a better term, I will call a fourth stylistic trend the communications age model. It is characterized by technological innovation that enables urban campuses to organize themselves so that they reach out in new and innovative ways. Telephone registration, electronic bulletin boards, computer interfacing of faculty and students, televised classes, video sections, voice mail, distance learning, libraries as electronic storers and transmitters of information, and a host of other technological devices are shaping the way campuses operate. While these are not limited to urban institutions, they are effectively enhancing and expanding the ways in which urban campuses deliver knowledge to people who may be spread out over many miles in the metropolitan geographic context. With the knowledge explosion and the rapid advancement of technology, one can only imagine what changes may yet shape the urban model. Already, rapid communications tools make it possible for faculty to link with students in their homes and in the workplace within a matter of seconds. This exciting new horizon offers great promise and is limited only by lack of imagination and financial constraints.

Walter Waetjen and John Muffo have called Berube's proposals of five years ago a "utopian vision of the urban university as a center for social action in righting the wrongs of the urban environment."[29] Characterizing urban institutions as "transitional," they noted that the difficulty in developing a feasible model has to do with the structuring of knowledge in the university and the way in which the academy is organized around highly specialized fields—colleges divided into departments, departments often divided into career concentrations, centers, or institutes with subsets of academic focus. This tendency, the authors point out, is not all bad, except that urban issues generally defy departmentalization. Waetjen and Muffo explain it this way:

Urban problems, more than likely, are ones that cut across broad fields or academic disciplines and do not lend themselves to study by fractionation of knowledge. The study of pollution of air and water is not limited to the discipline of biology or chemistry, but instantly becomes involved in corporate balance sheets, political considerations, manufacturing processes, and social concerns.[30]

Obviously, the search for new and more effective organizational structures will of necessity continue. However, since intellectual development and knowledge production are still the heart of the higher education enterprise, in the final analysis urban campuses are likely to evolve in patterns that are more like their sister institutions than they are different. The "ends" of all institutions of higher learning do, after all, tend to be similar; only the means to those ends are becoming quite different. And it is the means to the ends that will bring change. As Drucker has noted, even though McLuhan's much-quoted saying that "the medium is the message" is an exaggeration, the "medium" determines what can or cannot be sent and received.[31] Certainly, it is evident that the medium is changing. In fact, Drucker has predicted that just as the printed book became the "high tech" of the fifteenth century, so too will technological innovations of this era—computers, television, videos, and compact discs—have a profound impact on learning in this era.

Trachtenberg, in describing what universities will be like in the next millennium, said this:

> [A] century or two ago, much of what now seems so respectable within the university curriculum was regarded as the equivalent of so much Pac-Man and Donkey Kong. If universities survive the next two decades, and if they continue to adapt as they approach the year 2000, then we must be prepared to see them take directions that now look very unlikely or even bizarre.[32]

The challenges are as urgent today as those the nation faced more than 100 years ago. People have moved in great numbers from the pastoral settings of rural America to the teeming and competitive environment of the nation's cities. In a 1991 book sociologist Robert Bellah and others call for a communal effort to help build the "good society" our citizens deserve.[33] Kenneth Woodward in a *Newsweek* article reviewing the book says this:

> The good society is not the byproduct of autonomous individuals pursuing their own self-interest. Nor is it achieved by the careful balancing of competing interest groups. The common good, Bellah

reminds us, is the good we pursue in common. We may not agree on what a good society is, but the message here is that we will never have one until we realize that the public we complain about is us.[34]

Society is asking a great deal from its urban institutions. It turns to them for public service, for the development of new products, for the creation of an educated work force, for answers to critical social problems, for help with the environment, for nurturing of the arts, for transformation of the public schools. The order is a large one, and it is not likely to be filled in a few years. Neither will it be filled by institutional competitiveness nor territorial protectionism that places the more familiar models above the development of models needed to serve the common good. America needs its cities, for in them resides the greatest share of its largely untapped and undeveloped natural resource—the nation's enormous treasure in human intellect.

Will urban campuses be able to accomplish for urban America what the land-grant institutions accomplished for rural America? The answer, in large measure, will be determined by understanding and support within the academy itself and by the availability of adequate resources without. The land-grant institutions have provided an excellent role model. Like their predecessors, I believe, the "asphalt aggies," given half a chance, will lead the way to the "good society" in the twenty-first century.

REFERENCES

1. Stephen Joel Trachtenberg, "What Universities Will Be Like in the Year 2000," *Phi Delta Kappan* (January 1983): 327–30.
2. Ibid., 330.
3. Louis R. Holtzclaw, "Flexible Admission Practices for Adult Learners," *Lifelong Learning: An Omnibus of Practice and Research* 1 (Indiana University—Bloomington, 1988): 9–11.
4. Ibid., 11.
5. Faith G. Paul, "Access to College in a Public Policy Environment Supporting Both Opportunity and Selectivity," *American Journal of Education* (August 1990): 51. First published by the University of Chicago, 1990.
6. Ibid., 386.
7. Ibid., 387.
8. Ed Wiley III, "Cuts Leave CCs Underprepared to Deal with Growing Underclass," *Community College Week*, 16 September 1991, 1.
9. Ibid., 6.

10. Tom Morganthau and John McCormick, with Marc Levinson, "Are Cities Obsolete?" *Newsweek* 9 (September 1991): 43.
11. Ibid.
12. Jean Evangelauf, "Enrollment Projections Revived Upward in New Government Analysis," *Chronicle of Higher Education*, January 1992, A-1.
13. Ibid., 36.
14. Jerome M. Ziegler, "Winds of Change: The University in Search of Itself," *Metropolitan Universities* 1 (Fall/Winter 1990–91): 24.
15. Ibid.
16. Ibid.
17. Ibid.
18. Karen De Witt, "Universities Become Full Partners to Cities in South," *New York Times*, 13 August 1991, A-12.
19. Ibid.
20. Ernest A. Lynton and Sandra E. Elman, *New Priorities for the University* (San Francisco: Jossey-Bass, 1987), 29.
21. *To Secure the Blessings of Liberty* (report of the National Commission on the Role and Future of State Colleges and Universities, Terrell H. Bell, chair; American Association of State Colleges and Universities, Washington, DC, 1986).
22. "Marketing to Adult Learners," The College Board Office of Adult Learning Services, New York, NY, 1991.
23. *Time for Results: The Governors 1991 Report on Education*, Education Commission of the States, August 1986.
24. *To Secure the Blessings of Liberty*, 9.
25. Ernest Spaights, Harold Dixon, and Susan Nickolai, "Issues and Problems of the Urban University," *The Urban Review* 17, no. 1 (1985): 32.
26. J. Wade Gilley, *The Interactive University: A Source of American Revitalization* (Washington, DC: American Association of State Colleges and Universities, 1990), 24.
27. Maurice R. Berube, *The Urban University in America* (Westport, CT: Greenwood Press, 1978), discussed in Walter B. Waetjen and John A. Muffo, "The Urban University: Model for Actualization," *The Review of Higher Education* 6 (Spring 1983): 207–15.
28. Ibid.
29. Ibid.
30. Ibid.
31. Peter F. Drucker, *The New Realities* (New York: Harper & Row, 1989), 248–52.
32. Trachtenberg, "What Universities Will Be Like in the Year 2000," 328.

33. Robert N. Bellah et al., eds., *The Good Society* (New York: Knopf, 1991).

34. Kenneth L. Woodward, "Looking Past Number One," *Newsweek* (30 September 1991): 64–65.

EPILOGUE

❋ ❋ ❋ ❋ ❋ ❋ ❋ ❋

Author's Note: No book on urban higher education would be complete without the following description of the ways in which cities and universities are inextricably involved with one another. I am deeply grateful to the late Rev. Timothy Healy for permission to use these remarks, which were made at the 1985 commencement of Virginia Commonwealth University.

Big cities and universities go together and always have; the names Bologna, Padua and Paris show how true that is. Subsequent history is more varied. Oxford and Cambridge picked market towns in hope that they would grow, but only one did. Harvard bet on Boston and won; Yale on New Haven and lost. The tiny seaport whose name Georgetown stole grew into the nation's capital. So there may still be hope for Charlottesville.

At first blush what cities give to universities seems to outweigh what universities give back. The first gift is an infinite variety, since America's cities hold this nation's deepest wells of talent, and also hold, in uneasy peace, a rich mixture of colors, religions and origins. Another gift any city makes its university is its alternative rhythm. By that I don't mean the fifty-week year contrasted with the lazy rhythms of semesters and summer vacation. I mean rather the pressure, the hurry, the general fuss of business and commerce. The rhythms of trade and commerce impose themselves even on the life of the university, and once out of class its students face the hard and demanding deadlines of jobs.

Finally, the city never lets its universities escape its most priceless lesson, the correctives of facts and pain. Walk off the campus and you meet the "strained, time-ridden faces, distracted from distraction by distraction" that fill any city streets. A walk around any city can douse the ebullience of youth and curb the arrogance of learning. In all our streets we meet the myriad masks of God, but we find also in all of them God's own antidote against mistaking the generosity of the young for understanding, or the theoretical skill of the old for fact.

I grew up in two universities in the city of New York, Fordham and The City University. The city kept me always aware that both universities were meant to serve a world that moved "in appetency on its metalled ways." I was lucky, because as a priest I got to see the night face of the city:

the hospital nurse who'd call six hospitals at 2:00 A.M. to find a kid who was hurt; the policeman who'd run a one-way street in a squad car to get me there; the telephone operator who'd cut into a conversation so that I could tell of death; the rough kindness of the men in the morgue, who, because they offered a cup of coffee with gentleness and love, made it seem the Holy Grail. At night, among the many who help, one sees any great city ribbed and reeved in God's "strong toils of grace."

The strut and trade, however, do not move in only one direction. Virginia Commonwealth University serves its city and serves it well. It first feeds its endless demand for talent and skill. All universities use the same tools, the classic ones, but they are different in cities. A street-bred curiosity in both young and old add salt to all you do. The humanities gather to themselves the new energies of new people, a welcome to diversity that renews the imagination and sends it haring to find beauties where they were least expected. All around you lies the stuff of social science, the vast mix of a major American city with its problems and its triumphs. Richmond also teaches a history of struggle and defeat, but, like San Francisco and Chicago, it teaches the power of rising again from its ashes. All VCU's skills, all its tools, are involved in quiet labor at the job Alfred North Whitehead outlined for universities; by making citizens, particularly new ones, you quietly remake the city itself.

There are two urgent jobs that VCU, like all universities, both public and private, must do for the city in which it lives. The first is to restore for Richmond, and through it in part for the nation, our once full-powered urgency about integration as a necessary step in the struggle for racial justice. The second is the university's modern task of delivering a people, dinned into insensibility by the cacophony of modern communications, from the message that only the material matters.

Richmond, like any city, gathers the nation's excluded, whether the exclusion be because of race or poverty or both. The great glory of public education in America has been the steady expansion of opportunity for all people; the working out of the American dream that all talent should be placed at the nation's disposal and trained to the limit of its capacity. A university is one of the few places in a city's working life where the young of all colors and races work together in common patterns and through common rhythms. Within your walls you can, at times, make a model of what the city itself could look like. Here is Richmond's laboratory where young men and women of all races and languages ready themselves for service in tomorrow's America. You must make certain that access to that service is as all-inclusive as the rich life of the city itself.

The second major task that both public and private universities must face and face together is defensive. Even against the din of materialism, now aided and guided by a national government that preaches a gospel of material well-being, we must show the young that there are other choices. We who teach know this nation's greatest untapped resource is the idealism and generosity of the young. We also know that universities are the best places on earth to feed both. Our philosophers teach us that the struggle against racial injustice has justice itself, not industrial peace, as its object. Our historians can show us how and why America must stand for its dream of freedom and not for its awesome power, especially when that power is brought to bear upon the weak. Our social scientists know that cities must work, not because they concentrate markets, but because they are good places for men and women to live in. Our scientists are more aware within the academy than out of it that science is a servant, not a master, and even less a pandar to an adolescent instinct for power. Because we can bring the young together with their elders who are grave, wise, good and at times wild, we can help them rage against "the dying of the light."

We will, of course, no longer be able to do either job if the new-think from Washington has its way with universities in Virginia and elsewhere; if the small must go down before the large and the private before the public; if the elite must be saved for the rich and poor people cooled out altogether; if, most tragically of all, the freedom of students' choice that disciplines all of us must yield to an ideology of ledger sheets. The very men and women who once filled the air with wailing over Carter's Department of Education because it threatened a "Ministry of Culture" now urge on us their dream of standards, their shape for the curriculum, their preachments on patriotism, even the discovery that "the halt, the lame and the blind" are by some wrench in revelation both blameworthy and expendable.

Indeed, Washington these days seems bent on adding insult to injury. The recent thunderings of the Secretary of Education, that freedom of choice doesn't matter, or perhaps more accurately that it doesn't matter anymore, are as far off the mark as the Agnewesque rhetoric in which they were couched. In his assault upon the young, Mr. Bennett, like all pitchmen with a spurious product to sell, distorts the facts and patronizes his audience. The cuts he is proposing will hurt the poor more than the rich, and his comment about stereos and sports cars ignores the generosity of the young and tarnishes their idealism.

The only antidotes I know to such folly are learning and prayer. Since I gave up learning when I took a presidency, let me finish with a prayer stolen from a modern poet, David Jones. When he wrote the prayer he put it in the mouth of an ancient Briton adapting himself uneasily to Roman rule, not a bad image of how cities like Richmond react to Washington. The ancient Briton prays to the earth goddess native to his valley. His words could be the prayer of its citizen students to Virginia Commonwealth University.

Queen of the differentiated sites, let our cry come unto you.

In times of empire, save us from the guile of its agents.

When they narrowly number the souls of men,
    notch their tallies false, disorder what they have collated.

When they proscribe the diverse uses and impose the rootless
    uniformities, pray for us.

When they sit in council to liquidate the holy diversities,
    Mother of particular perfections,
    Queen of otherness,
    Mistress of asymmetry,
    Patroness of things counter, parti, pied, several,
    Protectress of things familiar and small,
    Receive our prayer.

When they come in the bland megapolitan light
    where no shadow is by day or night,
    Be our shadow.
    Empress of our labyrinth
    Keep our green valley.

Note: These extracts from Rev. Timothy Healy's memory of the poem "The Tutelar of the Place" by David Jones are reprinted here as they appeared in Rev. Healy's commencement speech. Readers will find the full extract from David Jones's poem reprinted in Appendix A.

APPENDIX
A
❋ ❋ ❋ ❋ ❋ ❋ ❋

Extract from "The Tutelar of the Place"

The following is a complete extract from David Jones's poem "The Tutelar of the Place," on which Rev. Timothy Healy based the closing remarks of his commencement speech.

❋ ❋ ❋

Queen of the differentiated sites, administratrix of the demarcations, let our cry come unto you,
                In all times of imperium save us when the
mercatores come save us
                  from the guile of the *negotiatores* save us from the *missi*,
from the agents
             who think no shame
by inquest to audit what is shameful to tell
                    deliver us.
When they check their capitularies in their curias
                   confuse their reckonings.
When they narrowly assess the *trefydd*
                by hide and rod
                by *pentan* and pent
by impost and fee on beast-head
               and roof-tree
and number the souls of men
               notch their tallies false
disorder what they have collated.

When they proscribe the diverse uses and impose the
rootless uniformities, pray for us.
                    When they sit in *Consilium*
to liquidate the holy diversities
                    mother of particular perfections
                    queen of otherness
                    mistress of asymmetry
patroness of things counter, parti, pied, several
protectress of things known and handled
help of things familiar and small
                    wardress of the secret crevices
                    of things wrapped and hidden
mediatrix of all the deposits
                    margravine of the troia
empress of the labyrinth
                    receive our prayers.
When they escheat to the Ram
                         in the Ram's curia
the seisin where the naiad sings
                    above where the forked rod bends
or where the dark outcrop
                    tells on the hidden seam
pray for the green valley.
When they come with writs of oyer and terminer
                    to hear the false and
                    determine the evil
according to the advices of the Ram's magnates who serve the
Ram's wife, who write in the Ram's book of Death.
In the bland megalopolitan light
          where no shadow is by day or by night
be our shadow.

Note: This extract from the poem "The Tutelar of the Place" is reprinted from *The Sleeping Lord and Other Fragments* by David Jones, with permission from the publisher, Faber and Faber Ltd.

INDEX

❋ ❋ ❋ ❋ ❋ ❋ ❋ ❋ ❋

by Linda Williams